BIRDWATCHING

BIRDWATCHING

STEVE MADGE

Illustrated by
Colin Newman
Dee McLean

Consultant
Brian Hawkes

Kingfisher Books

First published in hardcover in 1980.
This edition published in 1986 by Kingfisher Books Limited
Elsley Court, 20-22 Great Titchfield Street, London W1P 7AD
A Grisewood & Dempsey Company

BRITISH LIBRARY CATALOGUING IN PUBLICATION DATA
Madge, Steve
   Birdwatching. – 2nd ed. – (A Kingfisher guide)
   1. Bird watching – Europe
   I. Title
   598'.07'2344   QL690.A1
   ISBN 0-86272-185-7

Edited by Christopher Tunney

Printed and bound in Italy by
Vallardi Industrie Grafiche S.p.A. Milan

Cover photograph:
Male chaffinch at nest

CONTENTS

Introduction

There are many hundreds of thousands of birdwatchers throughout the world who follow their pursuit avidly. However, if any of them were asked their reasons for going birdwatching, they would probably have difficulty in giving a complete answer. The reason is that there are so many varied facets to the study of birds, and watchers develop their interests and derive their pleasures in different ways.

It is hard to imagine a place where there are no birds. They are found even in the centres of our largest cities and in the most remote and apparently inhospitable wastes. It is possible for us to study birds wherever we find ourselves.

Most birdwatchers start their hobby simply by becoming interested in the beauty of bird colour and song. Once interest is aroused, they may want to know which species visit their gardens or the areas where they live, and, leading on from this, may wonder how the species populations alter from area to area. Then, perhaps, they may want to examine birds' breeding behaviour and other habits, and may study how the numbers of species vary from season to season.

Yet others may decide to study one species of bird in great depth, learning as much as possible about every aspect of its life. The bird they choose may be found locally, or travel may be involved.

These examples are just a few of the many forms that birdwatching can take, and it is up to the individual to choose his or her own level of study and enjoyment. It is a matter of personal preference how much time and money to devote.

Right: A familiar sight: a cock blackbird surveys his territory.

Opposite: A greater spotted woodpecker feeds its young.

Equipment

For birdwatching to be really enjoyable, certain basic equipment is necessary. This includes notebooks, binoculars, and, possibly, a camera and tape recorder if detailed studies are to be attempted. Suitable clothing is important, too, and bird recognition books will have to be bought or borrowed from a library.

Notebooks and Record Keeping

The birdwatcher should always carry a small pocket notebook and pencil. Though it is necessary to carry a penknife to keep the pencil sharp, a pencil is more convenient than a pen because it is easier to use in damp weather.

On every field trip, a watcher will discover things worthy of note. These may include descriptions of unfamiliar birds, calls, interesting behaviour, flock sizes, and sites visited.

After returning home, a birdwatcher should re-write his field notes into a more permanent diary or log. This will facilitate reference to the notes at a later date, and will prove especially valuable if the field book is lost at any time. A birdwatcher is wise always to write his name and address inside the cover of his field book in case of loss; someone may find and return it.

What to Record

When an unfamiliar bird is spotted, it should be recorded in as much detail as possible before an identification book is looked at. Points to be noted include size and shape – by comparison to a similar but familiar type of bird – whether its bill is slim or stout, and what tail, wing and rump patterns it has. The plumage should be described in detail, and also the bird's habits – how it feeds, and its call notes and flight action. The weather conditions and visibility should be noted, and the habitat and the time and date of the observation.

A rough sketch of the bird will help. It is easy enough to draw two ovals or circles for the head and body, and to add bill, wings, and tail. The sketch should indicate the position of markings or the distribution of colour.

It is important that the notes be made at the time of observation. It is surprising how easy it is to forget plumage detail and call transcriptions if making the notes is postponed until later.

Identification

After the description has been written, a bird identification book should be looked at in order to discover what the bird was. It may well happen that the most likely illustration in the book still does not seem exactly right. The accompanying text may help to clear up doubts, or other books may have to be consulted to confirm the identification.

Use of Notes

Soon, the birdwatcher will find that his notes are useful not only to himself but also to local and even national organizations. Most local ornithological or natural history societies publish an annual report, which summarizes observations made in the area.

Keeping accurate field descriptions is a useful exercise. Notes should be made at the time of sighting a bird, or as soon afterwards as possible – always before looking at a reference book. A rough sketch showing the outline of the bird with notes on plumage details is more valuable than a lengthy written description. The habitat, call, behaviour, and a comparison with more familiar species should also be noted.

11

Binoculars and Telescopes

The majority of birds tend to take fright if approached too closely. The details necessary to identify them cannot be seen unless binoculars are used.

Magnification

Not all binoculars are suitable for birdwatching, however, and it is necessary to think carefully before making a purchase. The most useful magnifications are ×8, ×9, and ×10. Anything less is not quite powerful enough, and higher magnifications exaggerate the user's involuntary movements – due to breathing and unsteadiness of the hand. A magnification of ×8 is best for woodland use, and ×10 is best for viewing open habitats.

Field of View and Bulk

The higher the magnification, the less the amount of light transmitted into the instrument. But this depends to some extent on the size of the objective lens – at the broader end of the binoculars. The greater the diameter of the objective lens, the wider the viewing area and the brighter the image. The diameter is indicated by the binoculars' specification. Common specifications are 8 × 30, 8 × 40, 9 × 35, and 10 × 50. The first figure in each specification is the magnifying power, and the second the diameter of the objective lens in millimetres.

Though an 8 × 40 has a wider field

A pair of binoculars with a magnification × 10 and an object lens of 50 mm is particularly useful for birdwatching in open country. The observer may prefer to use a smaller size in woodland habitats, where the birds will probably be nearer.

of view than an 8×30, it is a rather heavier instrument. A 10×50 will be bulkier than either; a wider objective lens is necessary to allow more light to enter. Weight is an important consideration if the binoculars are to be carried around the neck for prolonged periods. Anything above 10×50 is generally unsuitable owing to bulk, limited field of view (making it hard to follow a moving bird in foliage), and the overemphasis of any unsteadiness during viewing.

Price

Price is the next consideration. There are excellent binoculars available towards the cheaper end of the price range, but the more expensive ones are more strongly made, and are usually sealed against damp, and will probably last a lifetime if carefully used. If the amount of time spent in the field is likely to be limited, it may well

Telescopes mounted on tripods are essential for identifying birds at a distance. A panoramic field of view is useful when watching seabirds, or when counting migrating birds of prey.

be better to buy a cheaper pair. But it is always advisable to try them before making a decision.

Testing

Most shops will allow a prospective buyer to try binoculars in the street outside the shop. The glasses should be focused on a medium-distant fine subject, such as telegraph wires, to see whether the definition is good, and to make sure that there is no discoloration around the object being studied. Then the binoculars should be focused down as close as possible, because a birdwatcher often has to follow a bird creeping about in a bush or hedge at close quarters.

Telescopes

Most birdwatchers also use a telescope. Telescopes have the advantage of taking the powers of magnification from ×15 up to about ×50 for the more distant birds. Again, it is important to remember that the higher the power, the less the amount of light transmitted through the instrument. It is not worthwhile getting a telescope with an objective lens of less than 60 millimetres. To use a telescope effectively, a sturdy tripod is necessary; but cars and gate-posts will sometimes do to rest the instrument on.

Sound Recording

A small tape recorder is a very useful item of birdwatching equipment. It is extremely handy for dictating plumage descriptions whilst watching a bird, for describing behaviour patterns, and for counting bird flocks or seabird passages. It can also be used to attract other birds with pre-recorded calls, and is invaluable for recording bird song or calls in the field.

Choice of Recorders

As with photography, there is a

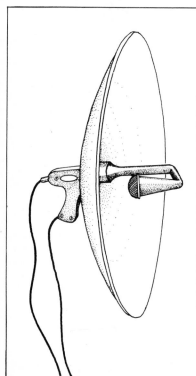

Parabolic Reflector

To amplify the sound being produced by a bird at the time of recording, a parabolic reflector is necessary. This is a bowl with a diameter of at least 0.5 metres (1.5 ft) at the centre of which a microphone can be mounted. The reflector is aimed at the source of the sounds to be recorded. It concentrates the sound waves into the centre of the bowl and hence into the microphone.

More sophisticated microphones and tape recorders do not require a reflector. But reflectors are almost always necessary when using rather less expensive equipment.

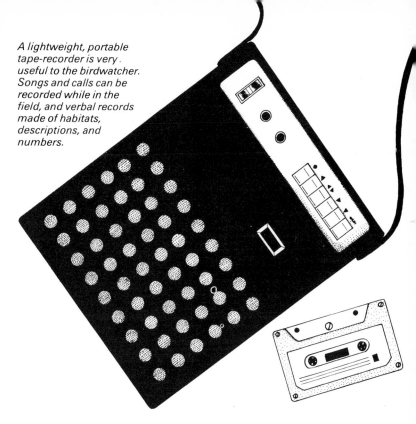

A lightweight, portable tape-recorder is very useful to the birdwatcher. Songs and calls can be recorded while in the field, and verbal records made of habitats, descriptions, and numbers.

variety of equipment available. The enthusiast is wise to consult other sound recordists for advice as to which make of recorder, microphone, or tape is most suitable for recording bird song. The Book List section on page 123 outlines in more detail the techniques and equipment suggested for making bird sound recordings.

Very good recordings can be obtained using relatively low-priced tape recorders, but care should be taken over the type of microphone used. Built-in microphones pick up the sound of the machine motor, therefore an external microphone may be necessary for clearer recordings.

By recording bird song, the enthusiast may make interesting discoveries. When playing back, individual birds can be distinguished by their song patterns and phrasing if the tape is slowed down. On holidays it will be possible to record the songs of familiar species and compare them with the songs of the birds at home. It will often be found that they are not the same. Many birds have regional variations in song— dialects in fact which make up a fascinating study.

In making recordings, it is necessary to take great care to ensure that the recording is not distorted by the sound of the wind.

15

Clothing

Provided that a certain amount of thought is given to it, clothing for birdwatching can be very much a matter of personal choice. Clothes should be comfortable and reasonably hard wearing. Obviously they should be cool in summer and warm in winter, as well as affording protection from wind, rain and cold. Inconspicuous colours are important – browns, greys, and dull greens being the most suitable.

Warm and Dry

Bright colours should be avoided at all costs. Jackets should have a number of large pockets for storing notebooks, field-guides, and other small items.

In winter, it is very important to be warm when watching birds in exposed positions. Thermal underwear is very useful, and it is better to have strong walking boots with two pairs of socks than Wellington boots, which can become damp and cold. Mittens are warmer than gloves, but can make binocular focusing a little difficult; which to wear is a matter of choice.

It can be very hard to find a completely waterproof garment. Most

Birds are naturally wary of the human shape. The birdwatcher should be as inconspicuous as possible – brightly-coloured clothes should be avoided. Earthy colours, such as grey, brown, and dark green, are the most suitable. Good use should be made of natural cover, such as bushes, trees, walls, and low banks, to conceal the birdwatcher.

lightweight rainwear tends to 'sweat' internally; it is also noisy, rustling with every movement. Such clothing is useful for emergency wear rather than for general use; it can be very welcome in cases of sudden rain storms or other particularly bad weather conditions.

A hat is useful to break up the outline of the observer: the human shape is well known to birds and they usually avoid it. Another desirable piece of equipment is a light-weight rucksack. It can be used to carry rainwear, camera, spare clothes, food, and so on. But it is sensible to avoid the temptation of carrying too much.

17

Photography

Fixed-lens cameras are adequate for habitat shots; but for photographing birds a telephoto lens of not less than 300 mm is essential.

A 35 mm Single Lens Reflex (SLR) that will accept interchangeable lenses is the camera best suited to bird photography.

Bird Photography

The camera has many uses in ornithology. It may be employed simply for recording habitats, right through to making intimate studies of the birds themselves.

Ciné or Still Photography?

Most photographers elect to start with still cameras, and then possibly graduate onto ciné work at a later date. Compared to still photography, ciné has disadvantages: it is more expensive, the equipment is bulkier and heavier, and filming and editing can be exacting and time-consuming. In view of this, most bird photographers prefer working with still single-lens-reflex cameras, usually using 35mm film.

Camera and Lenses

There is a tremendous variety of camera equipment available at a variety of prices. Although a camera with a fixed lens is adequate for general habitat shots, the bird photographer will really need to have a camera that will accept telephoto lenses. The most useful lenses are from 300 mm (which magnifies about 5 times) to 500 mm (about 9 times); but it must be remembered that the longer the focal length the more difficult it is to handle a camera with steadiness. The higher-powered lenses should ideally be used on a sturdy tripod to combat camera-shake; although this can also be overcome by using a cable release and a shoulder-rest rather similar to a rifle-stock in principle. A tele-converter is another useful item. It will double or even treble the power of the lens, though with resulting loss of light transmission and magnified unsteadiness.

Film

Black-and-white and colour trans-parency films are the most popular with bird photographers. Colour print film is more expensive to use in view of the amount of wastage necessary to obtain good photo-graphs, but transparencies may also have colour prints taken from them. When black-and-white film is used, the photographer can easily enlarge the image of the bird in his own darkroom. As fast shutter speeds have to be used in bird photogra-phy, the film needs to be fast. Films rated at 200 ASA or more are ideal for the birdwatcher's purpose.

Using the Camera

Using larger lenses needs practice. The camera must be held steady, and the photographer needs to be

relaxed when operating the shutter to prevent shake. It is a good idea to breathe out slowly whilst pressing the cable release or shutter if the camera is hand held or a shoulder-rest is being used. Gentle panning and shooting of a flying bird often produces better results than waiting for a bird to fly into the field of view. The depth of field (amount of the image in focus) may be rather limited with birds at close quarters. This must be remembered when photo-

A tripod or shoulder rest helps to keep the camera steady. The greater the magnification of the telephoto lens being used, the greater the amount of 'shake' transmitted when the photograph is being taken. Fast speed films – 200 ASA or more – should be used; with shutter speeds between 1/250th and 1/1000th to give sharp pictures.

graphing a moving bird, which may only have to hop or fly a very short distance before moving out of focus. The bird photographer must be prepared to waste a certain amount of film to obtain really good results.

Stalking or Hides?
Many of the good bird photographs that have been published are of birds at the nest. Nest photography should not be attempted by the amateur: it can cause stress to the birds or reveal the nest to predators. Parent birds may easily desert their nests after disturbance. In many countries, a permit is necessary to photograph certain species at the nest.

The Royal Society for the Protection of Birds produces a booklet entitled *Wild Birds and the Law*, which gives valuable information on this aspect of bird photography.

Bird photography away from the nest is perhaps more of a challenge. Setting up a small hide by a pool and sitting and waiting for birds to come to drink or bathe can be most rewarding. A car makes an excellent mobile hide: many birds can be approached closely and photographed through the window. Open stalking using bushes, walls, or hedges is rather more difficult; but excellent results can be obtained in this way.

A jack snipe caught and held for ringing. An ordinary lens is adequate when birds are at close hand.

A telephoto lens is essential for obtaining good photographs of birds at a distance. This Egyptian vulture was photographed with a 500 mm lens steadied with a shoulder-rest.

Fieldcraft

The essence of watching birds is to observe rather than be observed. Clothing should be inconspicuous in colour and blend with the environment. The birdwatcher's movements should be slow, with no sudden pointing motions.

The skilled observer will be able to walk slowly through woodlands without causing great alarm, using trees and bushes as cover to break up his outline. In open country, walls and rocky outcrops are useful as a means of cover, and walking on the skyline should be avoided.

By observing these simple rules, and by moving quietly, talking in a low voice to companions, and signalling by whistles rather than by voice to indicate finds, the observer will discover many interesting birds that would otherwise have taken fright. And he will be able to approach them more closely.

Listening for Calls

Identifying birds is much easier when the observer has learnt the calls and songs of the commoner species. This takes a little while, but the facility for learning calls grows with practice. A good way of starting is to try to track down any unfamiliar calls that are heard. Not all will be identified, but gradually the observer will get a sound knowledge of what birds are to be expected in each of the habitats visited. The presence of additional species will be indicated when new calls are heard; and more birds will be found in this way than would be possible if the observer had to rely on sight only.

Protecting Birds

The birdwatcher should realize how important it is to put the welfare of the birds before his own interests. He must never try to track down a bird to its nest if doing so entails disturbing the vegetation around the nest. Doing so may disclose the position of the nest to predators. If a bird is calling anxiously during the breeding season, the observer should move away; the bird may have a nest not far away containing hungry young or eggs that are uncovered. Fledged birds that are seen on the ground, apparently abandoned by their parents, should be left alone.

The Country Code

It is also important to remember to contact farmers and other land-owners before venturing onto private land. This courtesy will reap many rewards in the good relationship it will breed between land-owners and conservationists.

The birdwatcher, like others in the countryside, should follow the country code: Guard against all fire risks. Fasten all gates. Keep dogs under proper control. Keep to paths across farmland. Avoid damage to fences, hedges, and walls. Leave no litter. Safeguard water supplies. Protect wildlife, wild plants, and trees. Go carefully on country roads. Respect the life of the countryside.

Hides

Most of our birds may be observed without any need for concealment by stalking or by looking out over

Many nature reserves provide hides for use by visiting birdwatchers. From these hidden vantage points bird behaviour can be studied at close quarters. However, the field of vision overhead is very restricted, and birds in the air are easily missed.

It is important when watching birds to be as silent as possible. Sudden movements, or talking to a companion should be avoided. Brick walls make excellent 'hides' in open country; but a pair of binoculars suddenly appearing over a bare wall top would frighten any bird away!

open habitats. It is, however, possible to obtain closer views of many species if the observer is concealed in some way. Garden birds can be observed through the window of a house, and a car makes an excellent mobile hide. But the erection of a small hide will be an asset when the observer wishes to photograph birds or to study their behaviour without disturbing them in any way. A hide erected by a woodland pool, or near a clearing in a marsh or reed-bed, can result in all manner of interesting observations if the observer has the patience to sit and wait.

Instilling Confidence
Birds may sometimes be wary of a hide, especially when they see a person enter it. But if the hide is left standing, they soon become used to its presence. It is a good idea for an observer to have a companion walk to a hide with him. If the companion then leaves the hide and walks away

when the observer has settled down, birds will seem to feel that the hide is empty and will settle back to their normal activities. In other words, birds are unable to count!

It is also important to remember, when attempting to photograph nesting birds from a hide, that the hide should first be erected at some distance from the nest. It is then moved forward gradually over the space of several days to get the birds used to its presence.

Portable Hides

A small portable hide can be fairly easily constructed. It should be just large enough to allow the observer to sit inside it on a stool, with enough space to have an erected tripod in front of him. The camera lens or the telescope should not protrude too obtrusively from the viewing flaps.

If it does, the birds may well become uneasy.

It is possible to purchase small hides ready-made from firms that advertise in bird magazines. But a light frame, ideally of interlocking alloy poles, covered with sacking or similar lightweight brown or drab-coloured material will serve just as well. Holes for observation may be cut in the material, and the flaps held open with clips or ties. A portable toilet tent of the type used by campers can be converted into an excellent and serviceable hide by making viewing slots in the sides.

A small portable hide suitable for bird photography is fairly easy to construct. The framework for a camping toilet can be used, covered with dull-coloured waterproof material.

Bird Distribution

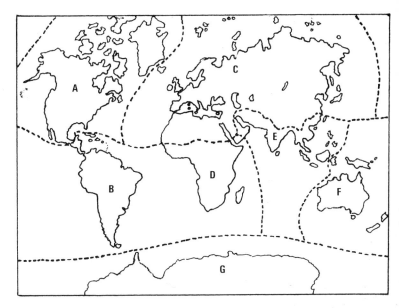

Bird Distribution

Although birds are mobile – and many are highly migratory – each species is restricted to defined areas of the world by particular environmental needs and geographical and evolutionary events. The limit of the range of a species is influenced by several factors: correct habitat, food supply, climate, geographical barriers, and competition with similar species.

Zoogeographical Regions

Bird distribution is a fascinating study, and a glance at distribution maps indicates that many birds share distribution patterns with other animals. The world ranges of birds and other animals fall into seven divisions, which are known as *Zoo-*

The Zoogeographical Regions of the world:
A *Nearctic*
B *Neo-tropical*
C *Palearctic*
D *Afro-tropical*
E *Oriental*
F *Australasian*
G *Antarctica*

geographical Regions or *Faunal Regions*: Palearctic (Europe, Asia, and North Africa north of the tropics), Nearctic (North America), Neo-tropical (South America), Atro-Tropical (Africa south of the Sahara), Oriental (India and South-East Asia), Australasian (Australia and adjoining islands), and Antarctica. The Palearctic and Nearctic are often combined as Holarctic: there are many affinities between animal families within the two.

Relict Species
Geographical events of ancient times have left scattered populations of certain species, presumed to have been formerly more widespread. These are referred to as 'relict' species.

Allopatric and Sympatric
Evolution has produced many similar forms of animal life; these forms take each other's place in different parts of the world. In some instances, ranges of similar species may have spread to meet each other over the course of time. Where ranges of two similar species meet, and they do not interbreed or normally occur within each other's range, they are said to be *allopatric*. Where their ranges overlap and they still behave as separate species, they are said to be *sympatric*.

The distribution of many species is slowly changing. Doubtless, there has always been continuous change. Factors affecting birds' environment – such as climate and changes made by human beings – cause certain forms to increase and others to decrease or even become extinct. Some 80 species have become extinct in various parts of the world since 1700, chiefly through the effects of human habitation. Others have spread considerably after adapting to live with man, or indirectly through the effects of cultivation or forest clearance.

Range Extent
Some birds, especially seabirds, may have a very limited range. The great shearwater, for example, breeds only on the island group of Tristan da Cunha in the South Atlantic; but it has a population there of about three million pairs. Others are found almost worldwide: the osprey, moorhen, and roseate tern breed over all the Zoogeographical regions except Antarctica.

The slender-billed gull is a relict species, breeding in scattered colonies from central Asia to the western Mediterranean and the Persian Gulf.

Bird Identification

The art of identifying birds in the field centres on the observer's ability to familiarize himself with the commoner species. He must also learn to recognize the variations of plumage that result from age, moult, and wear. Also essential is the capacity to identify the songs and calls of the birds normally found locally. Once an observer knows the commoner species, he will be able to locate or identify less familiar birds with greater confidence.

The beginner should not expect to be able to identify all the birds that are seen, merely those that 'oblige' with satisfactory views. Gradually, as the observer gains experience, he will learn the 'feel' of a species and will be able to identify birds in flight sufficiently well, and even to identify birds from their calls alone.

Each species is so distinct from others as to be readily identifiable – distinct not only in plumage but also in habits and voice. Some birds that are rather similar in appearance – for example, warblers and small waders – have markedly different calls or songs; so this is an important feature to be aware of.

When trying to identify an unfamiliar bird, the observer should take note of as much detail as possible. He should concentrate on size and shape, structural features, and calls as much as on plumage.

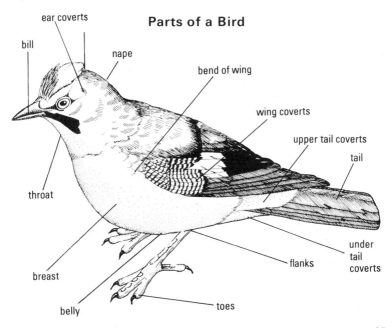

Parts of a Bird

ear coverts

bill

nape

bend of wing

wing coverts

upper tail coverts

tail

throat

under tail coverts

flanks

breast

belly

toes

A black-headed gull moulting its dark hood, thus acquiring a whitish head of winter plumage. The hood remains in a collar around the neck. In this state, an unsuspecting birdwatcher might think it was a Ross's gull, which also has a black neck collar in breeding plumage.

An incubating oystercatcher. Oystercatchers have diminished in number because of holiday-makers using the beaches on which they breed. Increasingly, they are breeding inland.

Habitats

Habitats are useful pointers to the identification of birds, particularly in the breeding season. Each species has its own particular type of habitat – the habitat best suited to it. For instance, a 'blackbird' in a moorland habitat is much more likely to be a ring ouzel; but a 'ring ouzel' in woodland is more likely to be a blackbird. Outside the breeding season, birds may be less strictly confined to a particular habitat. This is especially true of the migratory species, which are likely to turn up in all manner of strange places.

Each well-defined habitat has a particular selection of species living

in it. The main types of habitat are woodland, farmland, open moorland and grasslands, wetland and open water, coasts and estuaries, and upland or mountain; but there is gradation between a few of these and all habitats may be sub-divided.

Woodlands may be split into broad-leaved, coniferous, and scrub – or even further if necessary. Broad-leaved woodlands, for example, may be broken down into oak woods or beech woods or woods of whatever is the dominant tree. They can also be classified by size: they may be extensive forests or tiny copses.

Certain species of birds prefer woodland edges to the high trees in the centre of a wood, and vice versa. Similar things happen with the other major habitat groups, and this may be very important for finding particular birds.

Wetland habitats also offer interesting combinations of smaller habitats. Many factors influence them: whether streams and rivers are fast or slow, the type of fringe vegetation around a pool or lake, and the size and depth of a lake.

Change of Habitat

Outside the breeding season, many birds move or migrate to other habitats; these may be just as specific as their breeding habitats. Wading birds often breed by upland pools or bogs in the far north but spend their winter feeding on estuary mud flats or coastal beaches. Even here, each species will select certain feeding areas that suit its food requirements, and may differ from other similar species in this respect.

Size and Shape

On a number of occasions, a bird-watcher who has become familiar with the commoner birds will find that he is able to pick out something odd about the 'feel' of a bird: this is what is known as the 'jizz' in ornithological circles. Trying to identify flying birds brings this skill to the test. The 'jizz' centres around the general appearance of a bird. The way a bird behaves and subtle differences in structure when compared with other similar species give it a distinctive look that strikes the careful observer.

Distinctive Shapes

On the ground, some waders are particularly puzzling. They have a confusing variation of plumages in autumn – juveniles and adults, moulting from summer to winter dress, and so on. Getting to know the precise shape of several key species – such as a dunlin, a redshank, and a common sandpiper – will enable the observer to pick out the other species without having to flush them.

Ruff are problematical birds when not in full breeding plumage. They vary in size from being not much larger than dunlins to being bigger than redshanks. Their underparts may be whitish or warm buff and their legs anything from blackish to

Bird Shapes

duck

heron

robin

finch

owl

woodpecker

orange-red. But all ruff have a distinctive head shape: a smallish, rounded head and a rather short (for a wader) bill with a distinct decurve along its length. This head shape is different from that of redshanks, which some ruff resemble, and when learnt can be very useful.

The same applies to several other difficult groups of birds. Each species seems to have a 'facial expression' that is different from that of similar species. This may result from the crown being flat, steep, or rounded, the size of the eye being distinct, or the length and thickness of the bill being immediately recognizable.

On a more basic level, the first things to note when trying to identify an unfamiliar small bird is the shape of the bill: is it stout like that of a sparrow, or slim like that of a warbler? The structure of the bill gives strong clues, at least to the family to which the bird belongs.

The great white egret (left) and the cattle egret (right) are similar in plumage colour. But their structure and bill colour are distinctively different.

Comparative Size

Field guides give measurements as an aid to identification, though generally it is little help to know a bird's precise measurement while it is being observed in the field. However, measurements may be helpful in comparing the relative lengths of other similar species. There may be only a small difference in length between two species as given in an identification book, but the longer bird may also be considerably bulkier as a result; this would be readily observed in the field. It is important to compare the measurements given in a number of books, because authors have different methods of measuring birds.

Plumage Patterns

Birds of any particular species differ in plumage coloration or markings from birds of similar species. Those that live in open habitats – or who spend at least part of the year flocking – have diagnostic wing, tail, or rump patterns; care should be taken to note the extent of these. Usually, they have white markings that are useful in keeping the flock together when flushed, or that warn others of the same species of the presence of a predator. If, for example, a flock of chaffinches is feeding on the ground, and one bird becomes alarmed and flies off, the white wing and tail flashes immediately signal to the others that something is amiss.

Species Recognition

Waterfowl have distinctive wing patterns that help to keep each species together when a mixed flock of waterfowl is flushed. The birds fly up, and separate into smaller groups of particular species before heading away. There are many such examples.

Plumage Variations

Plumage varies according to age, sex, and wear. In many birds, the females are duller than the males, the drabber plumage being useful as camouflage whilst incubating the nest or attending fledglings. The males use their distinctive colours to attract mates by displaying; or to proclaim their territory to rival males.

Immature birds, even males, have a dull plumage resembling that of the female, and do not acquire their full colour until they are ready for breeding. In addition, a number of

species attain a distinct breeding plumage; this is lost in the moult that follows a breeding season. Although these variations may sound rather complicated, the observer should be able – with a little practice – to identify the majority of the birds likely to be found in a particular area.

Several species, particularly smaller perching birds, acquire breeding plumage in the spring through feather wear rather than by moult. The fresh plumage that appears during the autumn or winter may have the brightly coloured feathers obscured by brownish feather tips; these wear away by the following spring, and the birds bring out their full colour in time for attracting a mate in the breeding season.

In addition to the reasons for the types of plumage mentioned above, a few birds, mostly seabirds, may have more than one phase of colour in their plumage. The reasons for this are not clearly understood; but the Arctic and pomarine skuas and the fulmar have dark and pale plumage types, and the guillemot has a variation known as the 'bridled' form, which has a pale spectacle around the eye.

A flock of sandwich terns including adults and juveniles. The young birds have shorter bills, and brown mottles on their wings and mantle.

Left: A breeding group of guillemots. Most seabirds have a two-tone dark and white plumage – the underside being pale. This gives them protection from underwater predators who mistake the pale colouring for the colour of the sky. Their darker plumage blends in well with the colour of the sea.

The plumage of the nightjar acts as a perfect camouflage. Nightjars are nocturnal birds, spending the day on the ground, well hidden from any predators.

Beaks

Birds have no teeth, but their beaks or bills have become adapted for different methods of feeding. Even amongst closely-related groups of birds, there is some diversity due to feeding adaptions; and bill length can be a quite useful aid in distinguishing certain species of waders, waterfowl, and warblers.

Waterbirds
Waterbirds have three main types of bill: stout and pointed bills for stabbing or catching fish or crabs, as in the case of divers; bills with serrations along the cutting edge of the mandibles for catching and holding fish, as in the case of the goosander and mergansers; and rather flattened bills with small plates for sifting water, as with most ducks.

Waders
Waders have long, slender bills for probing into mud. The various species have bill lengths or shapes adapted for picking from the surface or probing to varying depths. Predatory birds – such as hawks, falcons, vultures, and owls – have hooked bills for tearing flesh.

The bills of birds have developed to suit their feeding habits. Birds of prey have short, hooked bills to enable them to pluck and tear the flesh of their prey. Herons have long, stout, powerful bills for stabbing and holding fish. Waders use their long, slender bills for picking and probing the mud surface. The peculiar upturned bill of the avocet is used for skimming the mud surface, using side-to-side head movements. Thrushes and blackbirds have slim bills suited to feeding on worms and other invertebrates found amongst leaf litter on the woodland floor. Many passerines have short, stout bills for feeding on seeds and fruits. Blue tits have small, strong bills used to hammer small nuts and seeds. The slender, curved bill of the tree creeper is used to get at minute spiders and insects living in cracks in tree bark.

Stout Bills and Slim Bills
Stout bills will be found in seed-eating birds, such as finches and buntings, and the shape varies to accord with the type of seed each species favours. Slim bills characterize birds that feed on land invertebrates. Examples are thrushes, pipits, warblers, swallows, and larks.

Left: The dunlin, a typical wader, has a long slender bill and legs. Its food consists of minute invertebrates found in mud and shallow water.

Right: Puffins in breeding plumage. Later, the colourful bill sheath is lost, revealing a smaller, dusky grey bill. During courtship, a great deal of bill-nibbling occurs between partners.

Bill Shapes

heron

kestrel

blue tit

tree creeper

blackbird

avocet

Feet

Although there are several basic types of feet, differing in the position of the toes, the amount of webbing, and the length of claws, there is less variation than there is in bill structure. Most birds have four toes. In some groups, the hind toe may be vestigial or even absent. The toes are arranged three forward and one backwards in most groups, although some have two pointing each way – for example, cuckoos and woodpeckers. Some birds – for example, swifts – even have all four to the front. Ospreys and owls are able to move one of the front toes backwards or forwards at will. The ostrich is unique in having only two toes.

Waterbirds

Waterbirds have webs of skin between the toes to aid swimming. This adaption is taken further by grebes and divers; they also have the legs flattened to assist in propulsion, on the same principle as the oars of a rowing boat.

The osprey has a rough, spiny covering to its toes to enable it to grasp and carry a wriggling fish in flight. The tropical jacanas or lily-trotters have long, slender toes and claws which assist them in walking over floating vegetation in lakes and ponds.

A Puzzle

A peculiar adaption is found in herons, nightjars, and pratincoles. They have a serrated edge to one of the claws; its function is not understood although many theories have been put forward.

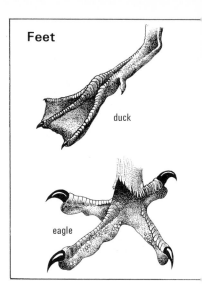

Feet

duck

eagle

Birds use their feet in a multitude of different ways. Waterfowl have complete webs between the main toes, and stout tarsi; these propel the bird through the water. Birds of prey use their feet to help to kill their prey; their toes are equipped with powerful, sharp claws and strong muscles. Grebes and divers have peculiar flattened tarsi and toes. The webs are not connected, and each flap of skin overlaps the other. This type of foot is very efficient for swimming: the action is similar to that of the oar of a boat. But the flattened legs are useless for walking on land. Perching birds have slender, well-developed toes, and use their feet for walking, hopping, and perching. Small birds that spend their time on the ground usually have an elongated hind-claw. This type of foot has good grasping power but would be a hindrance to perching birds. Several other families have feet with two toes directed forward and two backward; these are known as zygodactyl feet. Woodpeckers have such feet and very strong claws.

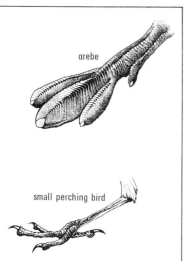

grebe

small perching bird

Webbed feet give waterfowl an efficient means to paddle speedily through the water. Webs of skin connect the main toes, and the toe joints are supple, enabling the webs and toes to be folded. As a result, there is little resistance to the water on the forward stroke, and on the back stroke the whole foot is spread open to propel the bird along the water surface.

The Woodpecker

Woodpeckers use their feet and tails when climbing. They grip a tree trunk or branch with their strong sharp claws and support themselves with their tails.

Flight Patterns

Identifying birds in flight relies on four factors:

1. Calls;
2. Shape of the bird;
3. Method of flight;
4. Markings on the wings, back and tail.

Calls

Very few species have calls that are used by other species in flight; finches and several other small birds, waders, terns, waterfowl, and herons have specific flight calls that greatly assist in identification. If the birds being observed are a gregarious species they may keep in contact with each other whilst on the wing, although others may be silent.

Shape

Concentration on shape is important; the observer should note how far the feet project beyond the tail, whether the wings are pointed or rounded at the tip, and the prominence and apparent length of head, neck, or bill. This last point is particularly useful when telling storks and cranes from herons; the latter fold their long necks back onto the shoulders when in full flight.

It should be possible, with practice, to identify birds down at least to family level by means of a combination of the above features. Identification will also be helped by noting how a bird is flying. Some small birds have a bounding or undulating flight – pipits and finches for instance. Others have a direct flight: starlings, some thrushes, pigeons, and crows are good examples.

Method of Flight

Some of the waders have distinct methods of flight, and woodcocks have a steady display flight, known as 'roding', over their woodland territories in summer. Snipe rise suddenly from almost underfoot, calling sharply and twisting and turning as they gain height. The low

Snow geese fly in formation. Geese, gulls, and other large, gregarious birds form straggling lines in zig-zag formations when flying long distances. Each bird is thought to take advantage of the slackness of air currents behind the bird it is following. The bird at the point of the 'V' or zig-zag is replaced regularly.

fluttering flight of a common sandpiper is quite unlike that of any other common small wader. The identification of many seabirds in flight will often depend on flight action rather than coloration: auks have a direct flight on fast wing beats, whereas the similarly-coloured Manx shearwater swings from side to side on stiff wings in between spells of flapping. The stiff wing beats of a fulmar are totally different from the looser beats of gulls.

Birds of prey can cause problems. Care should be taken to note whether the wings are held flat or angled upwards whilst soaring, or whether the bird hovers or is hunting by flying low and fast.

Markings

Many species have distinctive markings on their upper parts; these markings are useful to a bird in keeping contact with others of the same species. The markings can be in the form of flashes of colour on the wings or rump, or sides to the tail. The underwing colour may be important too, and with some waterfowl it is worth noting whether they have pale or dark bellies.

Buzzards make use of the warm air currents to assist their migration flight. When they reach the top of the rising thermal the birds will peel off in small groups, glide for a bit, lose height, and use their wings as sparingly as possible until they hit another thermal. In this way, they conserve as much energy as possible.

Calls and Songs

Learning the calls and songs of birds is very necessary to anyone wishing to become proficient in bird identification. Each species has a variety of calls that are used to express alarm, to contact others of the same species, or to proclaim territory.

Although all birds use vocalization to a certain extent, quite a number of species – particularly those of open habitats, such as seabirds or birds of prey – are relatively silent away from their breeding grounds. These birds are able to show their presence, instead of having to proclaim themselves as do birds that spend most of their lives in or near vegetation.

Certain species have a more complicated vocabulary than others. A single great tit may have as many as 40 distinct calls, although most species have a more limited repertoire.

Learning Bird Calls

The most effective way of learning bird calls is to track down and

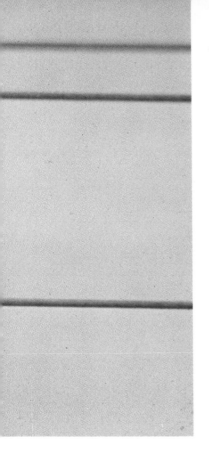

A male stonechat in song. Songs are used to proclaim a bird's territory and warn off trespassers. Ground-nesting species, such as the skylark, cannot always find suitable perches and often sing on the wing. Telegraph wires provide excellent song posts where there are no trees.

presence of a male bird in its territory, either to attract a mate or to keep out intruders of the same species. Song normally commences as the bird is setting up territory – which may be in late winter for resident birds – and continues throughout the breeding season.

Although bird song is normally only heard on the breeding grounds, some migrant species also sing while in passage or even in their winter quarters. But these songs lack the richness and variety of notes of the full songs, and are often referred to as 'sub-songs'.

Some birds are extremely similar in appearance to other species, but have very different calls and songs. This is often the case with small birds, such as warblers, which attract mates by using their songs rather than their plumage patterns. Chiff-chaffs and willow warblers have totally different songs but are virtually indistinguishable in the field otherwise. Certain African warblers known as *Cisticolas* – a fascinating group – are often only separable when singing.

Flocks of migrating birds often use calls to keep in contact with others of the same species. This is especially true when weather conditions are bad and could cause the flocks to split up.

identify a bird that is uttering an unfamiliar call. The call will then become more firmly fixed in the observer's memory than if it were learnt by listening to recordings of bird song.

Characteristics of Bird Song

Bird song consists of a set pattern of notes that is unique to a particular species. But there may be some slight variation within a species range; in other words, birds have dialects. Song is a method of proclaiming the

41

Migration

Most birds move about to a certain extent, even some of the flightless ones. Penguins are known to migrate by swimming, and some flying birds are known to move along part of their migratory route either on foot or by swimming. However, comparatively little study has been done on this aspect of migration.

The phenomenon of migration has intrigued people for many centuries. It was once thought that birds hibernated at the bottom of ponds or flew to the moon when they left their breeding quarters. We know far more about migration these days, although just how birds manage to navigate across the surface of the world is still very much a mystery.

Types of Migration

Some birds only move short distances. Young birds have to disperse to set up new territories, but this is hardly migration. There are several types of migration linked with movements from breeding quarters to winter quarters and vice versa. Altitudinal migration is characteristic of birds that nest in upland habitats, merely moving down to lower altitudes for the winter months. Weather movements relate to birds that have been moved out of their winter quarters by adverse conditions, such as prolonged frosts, snows, iced-over lakes, or natural disasters. Many seabirds lead a nomadic existence while away from their breeding grounds, wandering over the oceans in search of feeding areas. These movements follow patterns, however, and are by no means random.

A rather strange form of migration is found with birds that favour a particular type of food. Food sources – such as berries, seeds, and even small mammals – have good and bad years. Often, a run of good production or population increase is

A steppe eagle on its migration route. Its plumage is in a state known as 'arrested moult'. Moulting began before it left the breeding ground, but stopped during migration. It will continue again when the eagle reaches its winter quarters.

Right: Nutcrackers from the forests of Siberia depend on the seeds of the Arolla pine as their main source of food. If the seeds are not available, they must move away from their normal habitat. Sometimes they appear in countries where they are not usually seen. This movement is known as 'invasion' or 'irruption'.

followed by a bad season. Birds that have been dependent on these foods and have correspondingly increased their numbers then have to wander in search of food. Such wanderings will take large numbers of birds into areas where they do not normally occur. The birds are known to biologists as 'invasion species'; examples are crossbills, waxwings, nutcrackers, and snowy owls.

Long-distance Migration

More typical migration as we know it concerns birds that move considerable distances to their winter quarters. They have to move to find more profitable feeding grounds. Insectivorous birds leave their northern breeding grounds because insect life is minimal there in winter, and many seed-eaters also have to leave because of forthcoming snow cover. In countries that have mild weather, many birds are resident; their numbers may well be increased by birds from less clement lands coming for the winter. Most insect-eating birds move a long way south. Many European birds cross the Sahara to winter in tropical Africa, where insect food is abundant during

Sand martins gather on overhead wires. In late summer, the birds begin to congregate and build up in numbers, waiting until ready to migrate.

the months that are winter in Europe. Farther east, across Asia, many migrant birds move south into the tropics of India and South-East Asia.

Before leaving their breeding grounds, birds build up fat reserves to sustain them during their long flight. Some may even double their normal body weight for the journey. Many birds migrate both by night and day, although some travel only at specific hours: swallows and martins move chiefly by day, whereas warblers are mainly night migrants. The timing of migrations is critical: and birds will arrive on their breeding sites almost on the same day each year, and will come back annually to the same site to breed or winter.

Dangers of Migration
Migrants face many dangers: bad weather, long sea crossings, deserts, and mountains. Even lighthouses and oil flares are a hazard: they will draw night migrants into the glass or flames where many are killed. This destruction is compensated for by migrants rearing several broods of young on the breeding grounds.

Nests

Although many birds make no nest in the strict sense of the word, the nest is generally taken to mean a construction or a patch of ground in or on which the eggs are laid and the young birds reared. But birds make nests for other purposes, too – as roosting sites, for instance. Old nests may be used for roosting outside the breeding season.

For identification purposes, it is seldom necessary for a birdwatcher to be able to recognize a particular nest because, normally, a bird is in attendance. Many nests are hard to identify outside the breeding season when they are unoccupied; but some have a distinctive construction.

Making the Nest
Nests are constructed by either male or female, or by both, depending on the species. Each species has its own particular preferred kind of site. The type of construction varies tremendously, from simply a single egg laid on a bare cliff ledge – as in the case of the guillemot – through to a beautiful woven ball of feathers, lichens, and spiders' webs which might contain as many as 15 eggs of the long-tailed tit.

Holes in trees, cliffs, or walls are utilized by many species. These holes may be existing ones, or they may be excavated by the birds themselves, as is the habit of the woodpeckers. Nuthatches will adapt a natural hole by plastering up its mouth with mud until the most convenient size is attained.

An alternative to using a natural hole or excavating one, is to build a nest with a hole in the side. Examples are the ball of dead leaves with mossy inner lining of the wren; the ball of lichens of the long-tailed tit; the prickly sticks used by magpies; and the dried mud nest of house martins.

By far the commonest type of nest is the 'open-plan' construction. The 'roof' of the nest is open to the sitting bird.

It is normally the female that selects the nest size. But, in some species, the male may build several nests from which the female chooses one. This is the practice of wrens.

Other birds will utilize abandoned nests of other species. Old nests made by crows may be used by kestrels, long-eared owls, and even stock doves. The spotted flycatcher will occasionally construct its own nest inside an old thrush's nest, and the peculiar sites sometimes selected by robins and blackbirds are well known.

Nests at Breeding Time

It is most important to remember that the breeding season is a critical time for birds. The observer should leave breeding birds well alone, and refrain from disturbing them at the nest. Birds may leave their eggs or young when an observer is nearby, and there is a chance that these may become chilled.

Right: Grebes build floating nests of weeds, anchored to reeds to prevent them from floating away. The eggs are protected by a covering of weeds.

Right, below: The nest of a little grebe. Although the pale-coloured eggs are vulnerable in this state, when covered they will be quite safe.

Kestrels, other falcons, and some owls often use the old nest of a crow or bird of prey in which to raise their young.

In mid-summer most of the north European shelducks gather to moult in the Heligoland Bight region of north Germany.

Places to Find Birds

The beauty of birdwatching is that birds may be found almost anywhere, from the hearts of great cities to the remotest mountain tops. They are even found in deserts and way out over the oceans.

Unfortunately, over vast areas of the world's surface, natural habitats have been greatly affected by the spread of human habitations. Forests have been felled and turned into moorland, cities and roads have eaten up thousands of square miles of countryside, and in many places farming interests have become paramount. All these changes have contributed enormously to new developments in the distribution of birds.

Despite all the destruction and alteration in habitats, there are still many wild and remote places even in populous regions that support large numbers of different species.

As an example of the varied bird life of particular localities, the Scottish mountains contain not only several interesting birds of Arctic origin—ptarmigan, snow bunting, dotterel, and skuas—but also others with Mediterranean affinities.

The high Arctic lands are the home of ptarmigans. They feed on seeds of Arctic plants, burrowing under the snow in winter to reach the hidden food.

Bleak upland habitats are the territory of such birds as golden eagles who soar over the mountain tops. Wall creepers feed on vertical mountain faces; snow finches and Alpine accentors live on seeds and insects found among the boulder scree.

Coal spoil heaps, and other derelict land, can support a few birds. Little ringed plovers manage to breed in such places, and large numbers of roosting gulls can be spotted in slurry pools in the winter.

Towns and Gardens

Man has altered the distribution of birds and other forms of wildlife throughout the world. Either directly or indirectly, habitat destruction, cultivation, and the introduction of domesticated animals has changed natural distribution. Although many species have decreased as a result, a number of others have adapted to the changing environment and even increased through moving into gardens and townships.

Many of these are 'woodland-edge' species, which no doubt consider the scattered bushes and trees of gardens as being extensions of the edges of woodlands. Robins, blackbirds, thrushes, and tits are good examples.

Through the destruction of hedge-

rows with modern farming practices, a number of species are becoming more numerous in urban areas than they were even just 20 or 30 years ago. Magpies are known to be on the increase in this sort of situation, and in some towns their egg-stealing habits have even developed: they rob door-step egg cartons of their contents!

Tits and even great spotted woodpeckers have learnt to peck through

House martins are popular and frequent summer visitors. Their winter habits are more of a mystery as they are rarely spotted after having migrated to their African quarters. They may spend their time feeding on flying insects out of range of the human eye.

Feral pigeons are a common sight in many busy towns and cities. Their wild ancestors – rock doves – lived on rock cliffs. Tall buildings with numerous ledges provide a substitute for the natural perches of their forebears.

the caps of milk bottles to get at the head of the milk; this habit seems to be restricted to certain areas, although it is spreading.

Woodland and Cliff Birds

In some regions, wood pigeons and tawny owls have now become as much a feature of town parks as of the countryside. But not only woodland birds have moved into towns. Some of the most numerous town birds were originally cliff-haunting species. From a bird's point of view, buildings are merely cliffs with convenient ledges; no doubt cliffs were the original habitats of house sparrows, jackdaws, starlings, swallows, house martins, and swifts. In continental Europe, the black redstart often nests among the roofs of houses and other buildings, even in large housing estates. Its 'wild' habitats are mountain and sea cliffs. Starlings have spread widely over built-up areas in some countries. Their natural nesting sites are holes in trees and cliffs: buildings, once more, are useful substitutes.

The Collared Dove

The collared dove is an inhabitant of south-west Asia, perhaps emphasized by its pale, almost desert-like coloration. It suddenly started spreading from Turkey moving from town to town reaching Hungary in 1932, Germany in 1943, the Netherlands in 1947 and Britain in 1952. Now, it has even reached Iceland. This remarkable spread indicates how a species suddenly adapts to exploit a man-made environment. It has few barriers to check its increase.

Winter in the Garden

During the winter months, many birds leave woodlands and roam in search of food through gardens, much to the delight of 'armchair' birdwatchers. All sorts of birds can be seen if a well-stocked bird table is kept topped up with food.

Blackbirds are frequent visitors to gardens. In winter, they often rely for survival on scraps of food left out for them.

Starlings are common in many countries. But at one time their numbers were declining rapidly. Then, they started to become numerous again. Today, there are so many that it is hard to imagine that they have had a fight to survive.

Left: Blue tits are regular visitors to the garden bird table, although ringing has shown that large numbers also move through town areas. They feed their young almost exclusively on the green caterpillars of one particular species of moth, the oak tortrix.

Far left: Robins are popular garden visitors, in spite of their cheekiness. They are defensive of their territory, and skirmishes between rivals can become quite heated – fights to the death have been recorded.

Farmland

Formerly much of what is now good farmland was covered in forests or marshland. Over the centuries, the forests were felled and the marshes drained to provide land to grow crops and rear animals.

Farmland basically provides a variety of habitat types for birds. Relicts of the ancient forests survive in patches, and there are numerous small woods and copses that provide shelter for grazing animals and good habitats for such 'woodland edge' birds as blackbirds, robins, warblers, and tits.

Hedges

Hedges provide a similar service. The undergrowth at the bases of hedges is a tangled mass of brambles, nettles, and grasses – all

Open farmland seldom provides an ideal habitat for birdlife. Intensive crop-spraying destroys many insects and wild plants, leaving the birds little to feed on. Hedges are kept closely trimmed, destroying the chances of keeping nests hidden in the breeding season; and often long hedges are completely destroyed to make larger fields. But the dense hedges and tangled undergrowth that remain provide nesting cover for a large variety of species.

Tree sparrows prefer to feed in fields, and nest in holes in trees in small belts of woodland. In this respect they differ from their close relatives the house sparrows – usually seen in gardens.

of which have berries, seeds, or insects for birds to feed upon. White-throats love this sort of place and have a country name of 'nettle-creeper'. Yellowhammers, reed buntings, and finches are hedgerow birds, the reed bunting having spread out from a wetland habitat to colonize overgrown ditches and banks in quite dry places. This is a good example of how certain species can adapt to a changing environment.

Roadside verges are normally an extension of the hedgerow vegetation. They contribute greatly to helping wildlife in situations where other habitats are being destroyed.

Effects of Agriculture

Unfortunately, the economics of farming has drastic effects on wild-life. The modern trends towards intensive rearing of animals indoors, and the creation of huge mono-cultures of crops with associated hedge destruction, drainage, and crop spraying, make the country-side a very sterile place for birds to inhabit.

Crop spraying destroys insects and weeds, both of which are good food sources for birds. In the late summer and autumn, finches flock to feed on weed seeds. Goldfinches are a beauti-ful sight as they flutter about fluffy seed heads of thistles. Gamebirds, especially partridges, rely on insects to rear their chicks. Their popu-lations have markedly decreased in many areas.

After Harvest

After harvest, flocks of rooks and

Wood pigeons are abundant in rural areas, but also appear in many town parks. They feed on farmland, and roost and nest in neighbouring woods. Because of the damage they cause to crops, they have become one of the most serious pests to farming.

Ploughing attracts large numbers of gulls – particularly the black-headed gull. The newly turned soil brings worms to the surface.

Rooks are sociable birds, breeding in colonies in tall tree tops. They assist the farmer by eating leatherjackets – larvae of the crane-fly – a serious pest to crops.

jackdaws form to feed on the stubble fields. Many other birds, such as starlings and house and tree sparrows, form flocks with the large numbers of young birds having recently left their nests.

In some places, geese flock onto farmland during the winter months, feeding on stubble and potato and carrot fields. They are joined during the early winter by many dabbling duck, principally mallard and teal, which feed on grains of corn that have been left after harvest.

Areas of open cultivation provide good habitats for small mammals, particularly the short-tailed voles that are the main standby for kestrels and barn owls. During the winter months, short-eared owls and hen harriers may come down from the moorlands to feed over open farmland.

Woodland

Woodland habitats are rather complex and hold a marvellous variety of birdlife. Hundreds of years ago, many areas that are now farmland or are industrialized were covered by forests. But the trees have been gradually felled by man until in modern times only a few relict forests or regenerated areas of woodland are left. Yet other woodlands have been artificially planted by man for timber 'farming'.

Today many of the larger animals of woodlands have long gone, having been wiped out by man – wild boar, bear, lynx, and wolf. However, generally speaking, bird life remains, and is varied and equally exciting.

Types of Woodland

There are several types of woodlands. One classification is as follows:

1. Carr (fen woodland);
2. Pioneer scrub;
3. Mixed woodland;
4. Uneven-aged coniferous plantation;
5. Even-aged coniferous plantation;
6. Broad-leaved woodland.

Most woodlands show a mixture of these types, from pioneer scrub – regenerating areas that have been felled – to mature broad-leaved sections that may have been untouched for centuries. A good woodland for wildlife will consist of three main layers: the ground layer of low plants and ferns; a shrub layer of bushes and young trees; and finally the canopy of the trees themselves.

The long-eared owl lives mainly in coniferous woodland. It often breeds in old crow's nests and sometimes nests on the ground. Its long 'ears' are merely tufts of feathers; the real ears are below, and just behind the eyes.

The lower layers of woodland need small clearings to encourage undergrowth and young trees, and will ideally have a number of fallen branches or trees that are decaying through the activities of invertebrates and fungi. The invertebrate life of woodlands, feeding on these old stumps, on the leaves of the various undergrowth plants, and on the main trees themselves, supply birds with an enormous variety of food.

Other birds will feed on the seeds and fruits of the plants and trees. The older trees and dead stumps provide holes for birds to nest in. The oak woods that cover most of Europe and are well known to support a great variety of insect life, are exceedingly good woodlands for birdlife.

Birds of the Woodlands

Typical oak-woodland birds are hole-nesters: great and spotted woodpecker, pied flycatcher, redstart, nuthatch, tree creeper, and several species of tits. In some

The insects living in trees on woodland areas support a wide variety of bird life – especially warblers. Good woodlands for birds have extensive patches of undergrowth. Since these patches can exist only where there is a break in the tree canopy to allow sunlight through, the highest density of bird life tends to be around woodland edges and clearings.

places, birdwatchers associate a number of birds of prey with oak woods. They include buzzard, red kite, and even the rare honey buzzard.

Although many species of warblers are woodland birds, they show preference for life in the shrub layers and canopy about the edges of woods rather than in the thick of the woods themselves. By opening up clearings in woodlands, conservationists can increase the populations of these birds to give more of an 'edge-effect' to the forests.

Many now familiar garden birds were formerly, and still are, woodland-edge birds. Gardens merely increase the amount of suitable habitat for them.

Native broad-leaved woodlands other than oak are also very good for birds. There is normally little undergrowth in beech woods, and consequently there is little cover for ground-loving birds. Wood warblers are typical birds of beech forests, and in winter flocks of chaffinches

Birches are the first trees to recolonize a deforested area. Their speedy growth ensures shelter for other slower-growing trees. They hold a good variety of insect life, and several birds, such as redpolls, are attracted to their seeds.

Goldcrests are the smallest birds in Europe. Their favourite habitat is coniferous forest; and their numbers have increased with the extensive planting of new coniferous trees.

and bramblings feed on the fallen nuts (beech mast).

Birch woods normally occur where an area has been de-forested at one time. Birch is often the first tree to come back; and, being fast growing, it rapidly takes over, supplying protection for more slow-growing young broad-leaved trees such as oak. Eventually, the birches will give way to these slower trees. Birches are therefore the first stage in the recolonization of an area after it has been felled. The seeds of birches are very attractive to redpolls, and the sparse canopy gives an edge-effect that is attractive to

warblers, particularly willow warblers.

Wetlands

In wetland habitats that are drying out, willow and alder grow in profusion and help in converting swamps to woodland. This fen type of woodland is also very good for bird life. Siskins love to feed on alder seeds in winter, and willows are attractive to many warblers.

Coniferous Woods

In native coniferous woodland several very interesting birds may be found. In Britain, crested tits – which

Jays are colourful members of the crow family. They prefer oak woodlands, which they help to propagate by burying acorns in autumn to use as food during the winter months. More often than not, they forget where the acorns were stored.

Blackcaps have a beautiful warbling song, similar to that of their close relatives, the garden warblers.

are quite widespread in continental Europe – are confined to these ancient forests. An exotic-looking grouse, the capercaillie, is now fairly numerous in such forests in Scotland, feeding mainly on conifer shoots and various seeds and berries. Chaffinches abound in native coniferous forests as do many other familiar birds.

In some places, conifers are planted as a commercial crop because they are fast-growing softwood trees that do well on poor soils. The tree that does best for this type of 'farming' is the Sitka spruce which is native to the west coast of North America. Alien plants and trees do not support a great variety of insect life, and many plantations have trees growing so close together that no undergrowth can survive. However, the edges of such plantations provide cover for small mammals, particularly short-tailed voles, which are the chief food item of short-eared owls.

The young plantations allow undergrowth to develop for several years at least. They may hold whinchats and even hen harriers. The trees themselves have been colonized by redpolls, goldcrests, coal tits, and the common crossbill.

Heathland

Lowland heaths are a unique habitat of sandy soils, and have their own typical plant life and associated insect life. But most such areas are under threat from the pressures of farming. With the need to turn more and more land into farmland, many heaths have already been ploughed up and artificially fertilized, and the precious wildlife communities lost.

The typical vegetation of heathland today is a broad covering of heather, broken up by patches of gorse and Scots pine. Many heaths have been planted thickly with conifers, and, as a result, much open heathland has disappeared. The conifers have been colonized by redpolls, crossbills, coal tits, and goldcrests. Montagu's harriers have bred in some of the young plantations.

A number of species of birds are restricted to heathland habitats. The stone curlew or thick-knee was formerly fairly widespread in some areas, but it has gradually decreased over the past hundred years or so. The decrease is partly due to aforestation of the open heath and downlands.

Warblers

Dartford warblers are confined to certain heaths. Their requirements seem to be open heath with clumps of gorse and scattered Scots pines.

Lowland heaths are characterized by scattered patches of birches, Scots pines, and gorse. Large tracts of heather are also found.

In Britain, they are the only resident warblers, and being insect-eaters lead rather precarious lives during long spells of cold weather, particularly if there is much snow. The population wavers between as few as a dozen pairs after a severe winter to as many as 500 after several mild ones. The birds' recovery after severe winters is remarkably swift.

Shrikes and Hobbies

The red-backed shrike is also on the way out as a breeding species in some parts of Europe. Formerly quite widespread, this summer visitor has now decreased sharply in numbers. The reasons for the decrease are not really known, but are thought to be climatic changes.

Another scarce bird, the hobby, breeds in small numbers. It is a summer visitor to Europe, and feeds largely on flying insects and small birds, particularly swallows and martins.

The Nightjar

A more widespread heathland bird, the nightjar, is also a summer visitor. It breeds in forestry plantations, downlands, and coastal dunes. It is a difficult bird to see because of its nocturnal habits. But the distinctive 'churring' song is almost unmistakable. It is similar to, but louder than, the song of another species that occurs in this habitat, the grasshopper warbler.

Other Birds

There are many other birds of heath and downlands. Whinchats, whitethroats, linnets, green woodpeckers, willow warblers, and cuckoos are prominent species. And great grey shrikes may turn up in the winter.

The linnet is one of the most abundant species in gorse-covered country. The birds breed in loose colonies and form small flocks outside the breeding season.

Whitethroats spend the winter in Africa. A series of severe droughts in their winter quarters in the 1960s caused a tremendous drop in the breeding population.

Cuckoos favour the broken woodlands and scrub of heathlands. They lay their eggs in other birds' nests, thus avoiding all parental responsibilities.

Mountain and Moorland

Heather-covered moorlands differ from lowland heaths not only in being higher, but also in being colder and relatively treeless – although many areas now have plantations of conifers, particularly sitka spruce and larch. Gullies and streams have small stands of rowans, the berries of which are attractive to thrushes and ring ouzels in the autumn.

The most obvious bird of heather moors is the grouse. The red grouse, which was at one time thought to be endemic to Britain, is now known to be a subspecies of the willow grouse of Scandinavia. It feeds on shoots and seeds of heather, and berries of other upland plants in autumn. A popular game-bird, its habitat is artificially controlled for shooting interests in many areas. Some heather moors are burnt in rotation to prevent the heather from becoming too dense and woody; the recolonizing heather shoots provide food for grouse. Other plants, such as bilberry, spring up over the more open ground, until the heather again becomes bushy. Unfortunately, the measures taken to protect game-birds by gamekeepers have included the destruction of upland predatory birds. Conservation laws have to some extent stopped this destruction and the numbers of predatory birds have increased; but it is not always easy to enforce conservation regulations.

Although heather may be dominant on acidic moorland, there will also be extensive grassy hollows, sphagnum bogs, and rocky outcrops. Meadow pipits abound in such places, being the typical small bird

Curlews are very much at home in moorland bog habitats. Their well-known trilling calls are used in flight to indicate the boundaries of their territory.

Open upland habitats are used by many bird species during the breeding season, but are usually forsaken during the bleak winter months. A few stalwarts, such as the red grouse, may be found throughout the year.

Hooded crows can be found in upland districts of northern Scotland, the Isle of Man, and throughout Ireland. The carrion crow, a member of the same species, is absent from all these areas.

of the uplands. Small parties of young birds are a feature of late summer before they forsake the moorlands for lower altitudes. Twite can be common on certain uplands, though they have a preference for pastures and the edges of the heather moors and are not found in all moorland areas. In some places, they remain throughout the winter, feeding on lower pastures. Elsewhere, they leave the uplands and move down to coastal fields and saltmarshes.

Birds of Prey

The hen harrier hunts low over many northern moors. Helped by conservancy laws, it has spread to new areas, though its colonization of some sites has been hampered by illegal persecution on grouse moors. A small falcon has also increased in numbers because of protection; the merlin nests either on the ground among heather or in old nests of crows in isolated trees. It feeds on small birds, particularly meadow pipits, but, like its prey, forsakes the uplands in winter, moving down to coasts and estuaries. The short-eared owl is the most raptor-like of the owls, often hunting by day,

flying low and harrier-like on long wings, looking out for small mammals, particularly voles.

The planting of conifers on uplands has benefited the predatory birds: their prey finds nesting cover and sheltered grassland along the rides of the plantations. The fact that heather burning does not take place close to these plantations also helps in providing cover.

Spring on the Moors

In the spring, moorlands resound to the haunting calls of waders travelling from the estuaries to breed. Most waders breed by the Arctic tundra bogs and pools, taking advantage of the myriads of midges and other insects that abound in the short Arctic summer. A few species breed on European moorlands: the wetter parts, bogs and pool edges, are favoured. Curlews bubble, golden plovers echo their mournful whistles, and dunlin trill about the mosses. Temminck's stints are fairly common in the uplands of Scandinavia. The stony shores of moorland streams are the preferred haunt of common sandpipers. Scotland has a few more breeding waders; greenshank breed on some of the higher moors, and in the extreme north whimbrel may be found.

Seabirds

Lesser black-backed gulls breed in small colonies on a few northern moorlands, while common and black-headed gulls form colonies about edges of upland pools and lochans. In the far north of Scotland, Arctic skuas and great skuas may frequently be found on coastal moors.

Special Habitats

Stone walls are an attractive feature of some uplands. These are popular haunts of wheatears and, in the west, stonechats. As altitude increases, heather thins out into rocky scree slopes and craggy peaks where some uncommon plants grow among the boulders.

The high hills and plateaus of Scandinavia, Scotland, Iceland, and Greenland have many affinities of bird and plant life. The golden eagle is found in many parts of Scotland: indeed, Scotland has perhaps one-third of the total European population of this magnificent bird. Its principal food is the blue hare, although red grouse and ptarmigan are important prey items in some districts.

Ptarmigan are mountain relatives of the red grouse, breeding among boulders and scree of high, remote mountain areas. In many parts of the Arctic, ptarmigan are the only birds to remain throughout the winter – even burrowing below the snow to feed on seeds of Arctic plants. Snow buntings breed in much the same habitats as ptarmigan, although they leave the mountains for coastal fields and shores during the bleak and frozen winter months.

Southern Europe

The mountains of southern Europe have several birds that are not found elsewhere in the continent. Alpine choughs are quite tame at some tourist resorts in the Alps, feeding on scraps thrown to them. Snow finches and even the exotic wall creeper may be found in the higher parts of the southern mountain chains. If the observer is very lucky, the rare lammergeier or bearded vulture may be discovered in the Pyrenees.

Dotterels are rare summer visitors to the highest peaks of mountains in Scotland. Unlike other birds, the female is more colourful than the male, and does all the courting and displaying. The male bird incubates the eggs and rears the young. This reversal of roles, rare in birds, is shared by the phalaropes.

Freshwater Marshes

The shores of freshwater lakes and ponds are usually partly fringed with beds of reeds, reedmace, or wet grassy meadows. The plant communities of these 'marshes' are interesting and quite complex. A lake's borders may have varying zones of vegetation, used by many different types of birds.

Along the edge of its open water, a lake will have beds of Phragmites, Glyceria, or Typha. The first is the most favoured by bird life, and is used by bearded reedlings, reed warblers, bitterns, marsh harriers, and Savi's warblers. Outside the breeding season, the tall vegetation provides excellent roost sites for numerous starlings, yellow wagtails, and swallows. Phragmites beds support large numbers of insects. Aphids, in particular, abound in the time when warblers are feeding-up to put on the fat that will sustain them whilst on their migratory travels.

Alder and willow scrub encroach into reed-beds as a stage of drying out the land. Once a bed has been established, the plants in it send roots out into the open water; gradually the dense root systems form a mat of vegetation to enable scrub to grow behind them. A noisy but very skulking little bird, Cetti's

Lowland marshes, drained to facilitate farming, are still subject to winter flooding. The water meadows that are formed are excellent habitats for wintering waterfowl, particularly the dabbling duck. In early spring, when the water subsides, conditions are ideal for several species of waders.

Extensive reed beds are formed in the shallow water of lowland lakes. These may eventually become dry as the dense rhizomes of the plants build up a layer of humus and tangled roots.

Redshanks breed on lowland marshes – preferring grassy saltmarshes and water meadows. They leave these grounds in late summer to settle in estuaries and coastal habitats for the winter months.

Reed warblers make attractive nests anchored to two or three reed stems. These are often used as foster homes for young cuckoos.

or used for producing hay. However, the winter rains bring floods and they may remain under water all winter. The value of these meadows to waterfowl is inestimable. Dabbling ducks are able to feed in the shallow water on the masses of plant seeds that have been left from the previous summer. Herds of Bewick's swans from Siberia winter in this type of habitat, in countries as far west as Britain.

When spring comes, the floods subside, leaving extensive areas of wet fields for breeding birds to come back to. These include snipe, redshank, lapwing, black-headed gulls, and, in a few places, such rare breeders as black-tailed godwit, ruff, and garganey.

Unfortunately water meadows and other marshy habitats are under pressure from human beings. In some countries, few extensive marshes remain; the marshland has been drained for farming interests.

warbler, may be found in this sort of habitat.

Moving onto drier land, a tangle of lower-growing plants, such as docks, willowherbs, sedges, and rushes – all good seed-bearing species – will be found growing. The seeds of these and other plants are very important to wildfowl during the winter months. Reed buntings, sedge warblers, moorhens, water rails, and grasshopper warblers breed in such places.

Water Meadows

Water meadows are low-lying fields that are usually dry in summer. Then, they may be grazed by cattle

Sand martins arrive in large numbers from their African winter quarters in early spring. They breed in colonies in holes in sandy river banks and gravel pits.

Great crested grebes were at one time persecuted because their feathers were a valued fashion item. Once they became a protected species, their population grew. Now they can be found in fairly large numbers on inland lowland lakes.

Kingfishers excavate nesting holes in sandy river banks, lining the nest chamber sparingly with a few fish bones. The breeding population is affected by severe winters when their feeding ground is frozen over for lengthy periods. In these conditions, the birds move down river until they reach estuaries or the coast.

Grey wagtails breed on fast-flowing streams and rivers, feeding by the edges of quieter stretches. They build their nests in nooks and crannies by the banks of rivers, under bridges, and in walls.

Rivers, Canals, and Lakes

Freshwater wetlands are under pressure as natural habitats because people frequent them for recreational reasons. Boating and fishing are popular pursuits that often compete with the interests of wildlife.

Lakes and waterways attract birdwatchers as much as they attract birds. They can be divided into a number of basic types:

1. Lowland rivers or streams;
2. Canals;
3. Upland rivers or streams;
4. Ditches;
5. Gravel pits;
6. Upland pools or tarns;
7. Reservoirs;
8. Lowland lakes;
9. Smaller pools or flood flashes.

Lowland Rivers and Canals

Slow-moving lowland rivers meander through fields and meadows. They are rich in aquatic plant life and carve low banks along their course. Sand martins nest in small colonies in these banks, and isolated pairs of kingfishers breed in similar situations. The vegetation along the edges of many such rivers (and also canals) holds sedge warblers and reed buntings. Pied wagtails usually nest and feed near slow rivers; but they are not restricted to this habitat outside the breeding season. Often a meandering river will leave small ponds in the form of 'ox-bow lakes'. These are inhabited by the same species, and will normally house a pair of mute swans, although these swans are often quite aggressive and may chase away other breeding waterfowl from the pool.

Canals are favoured haunts of

Floating aquatic plants provide a perfect breeding ground for invertebrate life. The vegetation also offers ideal nesting sites for water birds.

some waterfowl: moorhens, coots, great crested grebes, and little grebes. The last two species build floating nests of aquatic weeds that are often anchored to reed stems to prevent them floating away.

Upland Rivers

Upland rivers are fast-flowing and rush down from moorlands or mountains. The birds of such rivers are adapted to feeding along the stony banks and in tiny pools as well as on the swiftly-moving rivers themselves. The dipper is the classic bird of this situation. It is the only passerine bird that is truly aquatic in nature. It feeds by walking along the bottom of fast streams, and can then be seen emerging onto rocks and boulders to bob its body and flick its white eyelids. It eats invertebrates, particularly dragonfly larvae, and nests under the shade of river banks

Fast-flowing rivers are the haunt of dippers and grey wagtails. They feed on invertebrates found in the more sheltered pools at the sides of the river. The fast flow of the river prevents aquatic plants from establishing root in the loose stones of the river bed.

and bridges. Grey wagtails and common sandpipers breed in similar areas, although the latter are only summer visitors and prefer the more open-sided streams of the moorlands.

Upland Lakes

Upland lakes and reservoirs are generally very acidic and receive little in the way of nutrients from the surrounding poor soils. They are known as *oligotrophic lakes*, and are low in aquatic plant and animal life. Few birds frequent these lakes, and they support only small populations of waterbirds, chiefly fish-eating species such as goosander. During the winter months, however, they provide useful roosting sites for large numbers of gulls or – in some areas – geese, which feed away from the lake itself. Some conservationists regret that these lakes are not used more for recreational boating, and the lowland lakes left for wildlife.

Lowland Lakes

Lowland lakes receive drainage from productive soils containing a high level of nutrients. They are known as *eutrophic lakes* and are superb habitats for wildlife. Their very interesting plant and animal communities may be quite complex. The various types of fringe vegetation and marshes are rich in insect life, whereas the open water can hold a variety of aquatic plants, both floating and submerged. The water and muddy bottoms support masses of invertebrates and plankton.

Large numbers of birds feed and breed on these lakes. Waterfowl have two basic methods of feeding: either by diving or by dabbling on the surface and up-ending in shallow water. Comparatively few waterbirds are fish-eaters; the grebes, divers, and some diving ducks, herons, and kingfishers are exceptions. Fish are captured by diving from a perch (kingfishers) or by stalking and grasping (herons). But the art of fishing has been taken to extremes by the diving birds, which chase and catch fish underwater. In all cases, the fish have to be brought to the surface to be swallowed, and at this point the birds are often harried by gulls who hope either to snatch the fish or to irritate the diver into dropping it. Watching a grebe trying to swallow a large fish while noisy gulls dive-bomb it is quite a memorable experience. An interesting study of diving birds is to count and time the number of dives a bird makes, and to note how often it will come up with a fish. This study may be taken further by noting how successful young birds are at fishing, by comparison with adults.

Diving Waterfowl

Other diving waterfowl will favour parts of a lake shore where their food supply is most abundant; the various species will dive to feed on algae or shoots of aquatic plants or on mud-dwelling molluscs and other invertebrates. The dabbling ducks feed on seeds of waterplants that have been washed to the shore of a lake. Sometimes they actually pick the seeds from the plants. They will also up-end to get to shoots and root leaves. Mute swans are well-adapted to take this form of feeding: their long necks enable them to feed in deeper water than the dabbling ducks.

Swallows, Martins, and Swifts

Large numbers of swallows, martins, and swifts gather over lakes to feed on the myriads of hatching midges coming up from the lake; the larvae

Mute swans are aggressive birds, often chasing other waterfowl from their breeding ground. They pair for life, and usually nest in the same spot each year.

of these insects lead an aquatic existence. Lakes attract enormous numbers of such birds prior to migration, as they build up their fat-reserves before the long flight to Africa.

Gulls and Terns
Black-headed gulls breed chiefly by freshwater lakes and feed on the emerging insects. They are joined by little gulls and black terns during the spring and autumn migration.

During the winter months, large flocks of waterfowl gather on European waters in regions where the climate is mild. They have arrived from Iceland, Scandinavia, and other northern locations. Huge roosts of gulls come in to spend the night on the water.

Moorhens feed quite happily by picking food from the water surface, muddy margins, and even by 'grazing' in waterside fields.

Estuaries

Muddy and sandy estuaries or bays provide feeding and roosting sites for a great variety of bird life. Thousands of Arctic-breeding waders use estuaries as winter or passage homes outside the breeding season.

The best way of seeing the birds that inhabit estuaries is to find out where they roost at high tide, and watch from a high concealed site as the incoming tide pushes the birds onto remaining areas of mud. However, great care should be taken not to disturb the roosts. At low tide, the water channels on estuaries will hold diving birds such as duck and grebes. These are more scattered over the water surface once the tide has covered the mud.

Choice of Area

The birdwatcher will soon discover how each species of bird favours distinct areas of a given estuary. Although many waders are basically similar to each other, with longish slender bills and legs, each favours a particular type of food. By watching how each species feeds – some by picking, others by probing or dashing after tiny fish and crustaceans – one can understand how they live together without too much competition.

Flocks of wigeon and brent geese feed on a species of plant known as zostera or eel-grass; this is not, in fact, a grass at all. Zostera grows in extensive patches over the surface of mud.

The mud of an estuary is teeming with invertebrate life; many species of worms and molluscs live just below the surface. Some of the larger species, such as the lugworms,

Waders have slender bills, each species feeding in its own specialized way. Dowitchers appear annually as vagrants from their breeding grounds in North America. They have a particularly long bill, and this coupled with a peculiar jabbing action enables them to reach worms and other invertebrates living in deep mud.

may live some distance below the surface – just out of reach, even of a curlew.

On the surface of the mud, many other invertebrates live. A tiny shrimp known as corophium, a tiny snail called hydrobia, and small cockles as well as several species of small worms abound and are all surface-livers. They are food for several of the picking, rather than probing, waders.

Effect of Tides
The lives of the birds that inhabit the estuaries are governed more by tides than by daylight hours. They feed at low tide when the flats are exposed, and roost while their feeding areas are covered by water.

Upper Estuaries
Higher up estuaries, where there is some influence of freshwater, other species of birds may be found. Kingfishers and common sandpipers, outside the breeding season, feed in the streams coming onto the edge of mud flats. About the sides of the upper estuary, there are saltmarshes; these consist of the first stage of the drying-out of mud flats. A species of grass known as spartina grows on the mud and puts down enormous rooting systems. Gradually, various species of saltmarsh grasses grow after the spartina has formed beds. Once these have become established, farmers may well put sheep or cattle on to graze.

On the saltmarshes in winter, in certain areas, flocks of geese will graze. Barnacle, brent, white-fronted, and pink-fronted geese are typical estuary birds. During the spring and summer, a few species of waders – lapwing and redshank for example – breed on the saltmarshes. In the autumn and winter months, merlin and peregrine may be found hunting waders over some of the estuaries in the north and west.

The grey plover breeds in high Arctic regions, migrating in winter to estuaries throughout Europe. Its mellow whistling call is one of the most evocative sounds made by any wader.

Sea Coasts

A number of birds that now live in towns were formerly cliff-nesting species, both on the coast and inland. It is difficult to speculate just how house sparrows lived before human beings came on the scene and provided buildings. But in some places they breed in sea cliffs, and so do house martins, swifts, and even swallows. The street pigeon's true ancestor is the rock dove, which is purely a coastal species in some places, breeding on northern sea cliffs and islands. But the pure strain has been much weakened by interbreeding with domesticated colour varieties.

A small rocky islet is an ideal breeding site for many species of seabird. Predators are rare, and every available ledge and crack can be safely used by the birds.

Gulls build little in the form of a nest; the nesting platforms they use soon become flattened by the young birds. They always stay within their own territory, and if a young bird strays it may be attacked and killed.

Coastal Habitats

There are many kinds of habitats on sea coasts. They include tall cliffs for seabirds to use while breeding, shallow and deep bays for them to feed in, flat coastlines, and many large and small islands where seabirds may form colonies.

Seabirds are under pressure from man. Pollution of the seas, particularly by oil, has decimated the populations of some species, particularly the auks. The pressures of

Right, below: Shags use seaweed and other debris from the sea to build their nests. They prefer to nest in colonies, using caves or the shade of large boulders.

Sheer sea cliffs provide safe nesting sites for many seabirds. A variety of species may occupy the innumerable nooks and crannies.

species may be seen from other parts of a coastline outside the breeding season whilst on migration.

Other Birds

It is not only true seabirds that may be found about coastlines. Rock pipits are found along many coasts, and ravens and buzzards may breed in coastal areas. If a birdwatcher is really lucky, he might come upon a peregrine or a party of choughs. In some places, the green woodpecker is very much a coastal bird, breeding in rock crevices and feeding on cliff-top ant colonies. Jackdaws and tree sparrows and even stock doves are also found breeding in many cliffs.

During migration times, many small migrant birds can be found in coastal bushes. These can add greatly to the excitement of a day on the coast.

tourism, as well as cliff-climbing and other outdoor pursuits, have affected coastal bird life. In Britain, ringed plovers have almost disappeared from many areas as a breeding bird through disturbance of their beaches by holiday-makers.

Seabird Varieties

Many seabird species come to land only to breed, spending the rest of the year far out at sea. Storm petrels, Leach's petrels, and Manx shearwaters breed on small islands in some waters. Tall cliffs attract colonial nesting species, such as razorbills, puffins, guillemots, black guillemots, Arctic skuas, and great skuas. Terns breed on isolated beaches and islands and need to be free of disturbance. Many of these

Seawatching

Seawatching is a skilled and often rewarding pastime. Many birdwatchers become addicted to sitting on headlands gazing out to sea. Almost any bird can turn up under ideal viewing conditions. An autumn with northerly winds, following vigorous depressions crossing the Atlantic to displace mid-Atlantic feeding birds, would be a combination of events that seawatchers would find desirable.

Puffins are able to carry a number of fish in their bills at one time. They prefer to nest on isolated grass-topped islands, often creating a 'honeycomb' with their nest burrows.

An island seabird colony. Shags build their nests on large ledges or in caves. Kittiwakes prefer to build neat nests on tiny cliff ledges.

Common terns breed on isolated beaches and islands. In some areas the species breeds in inland gravel pits because the beaches are being used by holidaymakers.

Birds: Body Structure and Behaviour

Birds are among the most colourful and adaptable of the vertebrates. They are comparatively easy creatures to study, and their relationships with each other and with other animals are fascinating. They have complex behaviour patterns associated with breeding displays, nesting habits, migration, and vocalization. No less intriguing are their internal anatomy and flight adaptions.

Man has been fascinated by birds for thousands of years. Birds featured in several of the earliest religions. In ancient Egypt, the Sacred Ibis was worshipped. It can be seen in hieroglyphics and murals that still exist, even though the ibis is now extinct in Egypt. Today, birds are studied by millions of people throughout the world, and by both amateur and professional ornithologists.

Much can be discovered about birds by ringing them. Ringers have to be trained to operate nets and traps. By ringing birds, we can gain information about their population densities, affinities to wintering and breeding grounds, migration routes and methods, longevity, and fidelity to breeding partners. We can also discover the hazards and threats they have to face, and can sometimes take precautions.

Breeding Sites

It is known, for instance, that some species come back annually to the same nest site, and winter at another precise location several thousand miles away. Other species may breed in one country, migrate, and return to breed somewhere quite different from the place where they were hatched. Presumably, they have become mixed with flocks of the same species from another part of the world while in their winter quarters.

Longevity

The age to which birds live relates very much to their breeding success. Many small birds live only five or six years; but having several broods of young in a year compensates for losses in the population. Many young birds perish either to predators or while on migration; but one or two young from each pair survive.

Netting birds in order to ring them requires special training. Here, a rocket net was fired over the gulls while they were feeding.

Many larger birds have few predators. They tend to lay only few eggs and may not breed until five or six years old. Some wader and gull species are known to have reached the age of 30 years, but few small passerines reach a third of this life span.

Migration

Migration is still a mystery. Although we know far more about routes and how long it takes birds to reach their winter quarters, we do not really know how they navigate. There are several theories centring around magnetic forces, atmospheric pressures, and navigation by means of the stars or by following natural features such as mountain chains and coastlines. But our ignorance of migrational navigation is still the great gap in our knowledge of birds, despite the fact that migration is one of the most fascinating things about them.

Bird ringing assists the study of bird behaviour. In the case of large birds, such as the mute swan, lettered colour rings may be identified without the recapture of the birds.

Starlings form flocks in their thousands to roost in reed beds, woods, and buildings. They have been known to flatten completely a reed bed.

Anatomy

The body of a bird has the same basic structure as the bodies of other vertebrates – a strong skeleton of bones enclosing and protecting the vital organs. Attached to the skeleton are the muscles and other tissues, and the entire body is enveloped in an outer covering of skin in which the feathers are embedded. To achieve the lightness necessary for flight, many of the bones are either hollow or spongy. Though they are therefore much lighter than mammalian bones they lose little in strength.

Neck Vertebrae

The bird's head is carried on a column of strong, articulating verte- brae. In contrast to mammals, the number of neck vertebrae in birds is variable. A swan may have 25 but a sparrow only 16. By contrast, both man and the giraffe have only 7.

Wing and Leg Bones

The breast-bone, or sternum, has a very deep keel. This forms the anchorage for the powerful flight muscles. The 'forearm' of the bird is comprised of two bones, the radius and the ulna, which carry the secondary flight feathers that give 'lift'. The bones that correspond to our wrist and hand are, in birds, fused together. The thumb bears a group of feathers known as the *alula*, which are used for stabilizing flight,

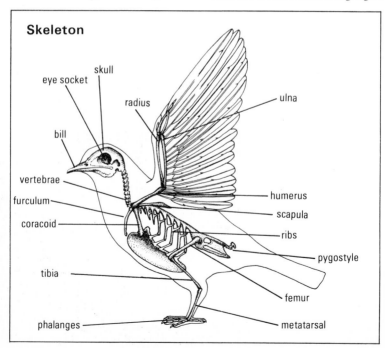

Skeleton

skull
eye socket
radius
ulna
bill
vertebrae
furculum
humerus
coracoid
scapula
ribs
pygostyle
tibia
femur
phalanges
metatarsal

Flight and Leg Muscles

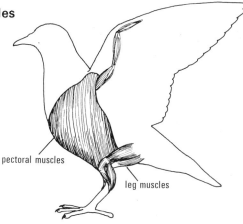

Great, sustained strength is needed to keep a bird's wings beating in flight. Large, powerful pectoral muscles, supported by the keeled breast bone, have been developed for this purpose. Similarly, the leg muscles have been designed to cushion the bird when landing.

pectoral muscles

leg muscles

particularly at low speeds. The 'finger' bones bear the primary flight feathers, used to propel the bird through the air.

To maintain balance, the leg bones are positioned very differently from those of mammals. This is necessary because of the weight of the massive flight muscles. The thigh bone is held almost parallel to the body, and what appears to be the thigh is actually the shin.

Pelvic Girdle and Tail
The organs of digestion, excretion, and reproduction are carried in the body cavity between the legs, and are to a large extent protected by the pelvic girdle. Beyond the girdle, the remaining vertebrae of the backbone are fused into the 'ploughshare' bone (pygostyle). This curiously shaped bone is important because it forms the anchorage for the tail and its muscles.

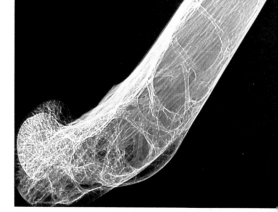

An X-ray photograph of a pelican bone shows the numerous air passages. These provide the lightness necessary to birds that spend much of their lives in the air.

Feathers

Feathers are peculiar to birds, and it is this characteristic which distinguishes them from all other living creatures. The feathers are a very lightweight, durable, and flexible outer covering to the bird's body. They trap countless pockets of air, and form a very efficient insulating layer. The feathers overlap each other very much like the slates on a roof; at their point of insertion into the skin they have a number of small muscles by which the bird can 'fluff up' or sleek down its plumage, and thus control its body temperature.

Structure

The feather is formed throughout of a dead substance called *keratin*. Branching off from either side of the elongated and tapering central shaft is a row of small barbs (*rami*), which are inclined towards the feather-tip. These barbs form the web (*vexillum*) of the feather. On either side of each barb is a row of minute barbules; those directed towards the tip have small projections, whilst those

along the underside are hooked. The barbules along the other side of the barb form ridges onto which the forward-pointing barbules hook. This arrangement gives lightness and strength to the web.

The central shaft of the feathers is composed of an upper, solid *rhachis*, and a lower, hollow *calamus*. The tiny hole at the upper end of the calamus is termed the *upper umbillicus*, whilst its opening at the lower end is known as the *lower umbillicus*.

Flight Feathers

The outermost wing-feathers (attached to the 'hand') are usually elongate, with the web of the leading edge much narrower than that of the trailing edge. They are termed the *primaries*. Their number is remark-

A feather consists of a central shaft or quill, with numerous barbs attached either side forming the vane. Barbules – tiny hooks – link each barb with its neighbour.

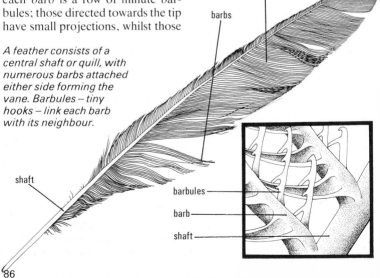

feather web

barbs

shaft

barbules

barb

shaft

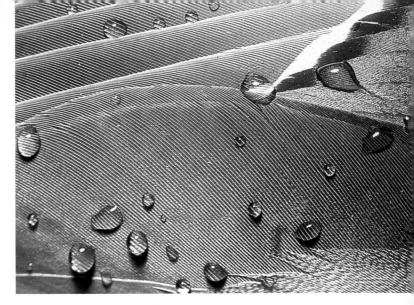

ably constant in most bird groups, totalling either 9, 10, 11, or 12. The outermost primary is almost always greatly reduced, and is non-functional.

The feathers attached to the 'arm' are termed the *secondaries*, and, in contrast to the primaries, have the web of approximately the same width on either side of the shaft. They also have a much greater range in number (6 to 32), apparently related to the length of the arm.

The term '*tertiaries*', applied to the feathers of the upper arm, has now virtually fallen into disuse. The wing-feathers covering the bases of the flight feathers are termed respectively the *primary coverts* and the *secondary coverts*.

Tail Feathers
The number of tail feathers, called the *retrices* (singular, *retrix*), also varies considerably. Some humming-birds have 4; some pheasants have 32. They are always paired, and they

The feathers of waterbirds are water-resistant. In addition, they help to conserve body heat and provide protection from the wind, and are sometimes used to attract a mate. They must be durable, as most birds only moult once or twice a year.

have associated coverts similar to those of flight feathers.

Body Feathers
The remaining feathers covering the body are termed *contour* feathers. They are arranged in definite rows (*tracts*), and are usually more rounded and softer than the other feathers. Their numbers (so far recorded) vary from the humming-bird's 940 to the whistling swan's 25,000.

Moult
As the bird goes about its daily life, its feathers become worn and damaged. Since feathers are dead, the only means of renewing damaged

plumage is by replacement, the new feather pushing out its predecessor. This process is termed the *moult*.

Moulting is, almost without exception, annual, usually following the breeding season. It usually commences with the innermost primary on each wing, gradually progressing outwards. About half-way through the primary moult, the secondaries also commence to moult, but inwards from the outermost. As the wing moult proceeds, the body feathers also moult, but again in an orderly fashion. At the same time, the tail feathers are shed, usually in pairs, starting from the centre. This method ensures that most birds have adequate powers of flight and body-covering at all times. Many aquatic birds lose all their wing feathers at once, and are thus rendered flightless for a short while.

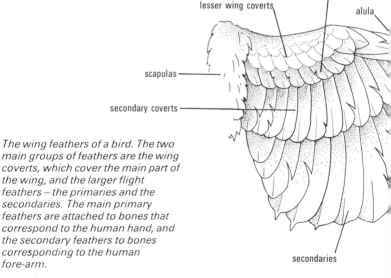

The wing feathers of a bird. The two main groups of feathers are the wing coverts, which cover the main part of the wing, and the larger flight feathers – the primaries and the secondaries. The main primary feathers are attached to bones that correspond to the human hand, and the secondary feathers to bones corresponding to the human fore-arm.

median wing coverts

lesser wing coverts

alula

scapulas

secondary coverts

secondaries

Wing Feathers

The care of feathers is important – preening and cleaning takes place regularly. Parasites, such as mites and ticks, attack feathers, and birds can be spotted scratching themselves to relieve this discomfort.

The waxwing is named after the waxy extensions of its secondary feathers.

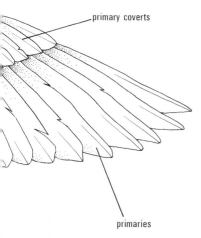

primary coverts

primaries

Flight

Birds have evolved the power of flight beyond any other vertebrates. Some species, such as swifts, have adapted to a life that is almost entirely airborne. Comparatively few birds are flightless.

How Birds Fly

Birds fly by 'swimming' through the air, using air currents for lift and manipulating the airflow through the primary feathers. In some of the larger birds, the primaries have slots in them to enable the bird to alter course with little effort, simply by opening or closing the wing tip slightly and moving its tail.

The wing is not completely flat, but is slightly curved on top. Air passing across the top of the wing has to move faster than that passing

How a Bird Flies

A bird makes full use of its wings to fly through the air; they are not merely flapped up and down, but used in a controlled and sensitive manner. During take-off the wings are lifted and brought down with a pushing action of the carpal joint towards the side of the body and out again on the up-stroke. The feet are used to push off from the ground.

A flamingo in full flight shows its well-streamlined body. The head is held slightly upwards to breast the flow of air currents. The legs are lined-up with the body to prevent drag.

In landing, the flight feathers are fully spread; tail depressed and spread; and feet extended to check speed. The legs and feet cushion the landing as the wings are brought back to the folded position.

beneath. This creates 'lift' that keeps the bird in the air. Air currents are used by some birds to soar and glide with little effort. The broad-winged birds of prey, and storks, pelicans, and many others, use thermals – warm air currents that rise over land – to soar on during the heat of the day.

This method of flight aids them during migration to or from their winter quarters. They fly by soaring upwards on thermals to a great height, peeling off at the top of the thermal to glide, gradually losing height, until they hit the next thermal; there the process is repeated. In this way, birds can travel long distances using little

energy; only the minimum amount of flapping is required. However, migrating birds have to land at night, moving on as the following day warms up and the thermals start again. And they cannot cross long stretches of water in this way, as thermals only rise from land.

A white stork brakes as it comes in to land on its nest. Its wings are spread as it 'back-pedals' to check its air speed. Its legs are dropped, ready for impact.

Use of the Tail
The tail is important to many birds as an aid to manoeuvring in the air. It is used both as a rudder and as a brake. By opening, closing, or twisting the tail, a soaring bird is able to alter course. When coming in to land, the tail is depressed and fanned to form a brake that checks flight speed.

Taking-off and Landing
Taking-off and landing need a bit of practice when young birds are learning to fly. Their antics are sometimes comical to watch. A number of water birds have some difficulty in taking to air, literally running along the surface of the water as they try and get enough 'lift' to rise into the air.

The Feet
The feet have to be tucked well up once the bird is in the air. They either fit snugly into the feathers of the under-tail coverts, or – in the case of some long-legged groups – trail behind the tail. Thus there is no disruption of a steady flow of air currents below the bird.

A gannet makes use of a strong up-draught of air that enables it to hang effortlessly.

A heron lands with its feet dangling to cushion the impact. The alula – small feathers at the bend of the wing – help the bird to manoeuvre as it lands, or to change direction in flight.

Senses

Birds have the senses of smell, taste, sight, hearing, and touch. But their senses have developed rather differently from those of human beings.

Smell

Birds use this sense very little, and it is not well developed except in a few species. As a consequence, some other senses have developed more acutely to facilitate the finding of food.

Taste

This sense is not very highly developed either, though birds do have a limited number of taste buds in the throat and at the base of the tongue. Like a number of other animals, birds avoid certain brightly-coloured insects which they know to have an unpleasant taste.

Sight

Birds have very large eyes in relation to head size, and sight is one of the most important avian senses. Because the eyes are so large, there is little room in the skull for muscles associated with eye movement. Birds therefore move their heads to keep objects in sight. Owls can move their necks through 270 degrees.

Birds that are vulnerable to predators have their eyes placed at the sides of the head to provide maximum vision ahead and behind. Most predatory birds have their eyes to the front of the head to pick out their prey. Birds with eyes at the side of the head have mainly monocular vision, whereas birds with eyes at the front and focusing together, rather like the eyes of human beings, have binocular vision.

It is generally believed that most diurnal (day) birds have colour vision and that nocturnal (night) birds do not. Colours perceived by birds are similar to those seen by human beings, though the eyesight of many birds is far superior to human vision. Birds have two eyelids, and have a transparent nictitating membrane that can be drawn across the surface of the eye to clean it without losing vision. It is believed that this membrane covers the eye while the bird is in flight as a form of protection against air currents that might dry out the cornea.

Hearing

This is also very well developed. Birds' ear holes are located at the sides of the head, just below the eyes, and can be seen if the feathers are parted. There are no external ear lobes: the 'ears' of a long-eared owl are merely tufts of feathers.

Instincts

Birds' instincts revolve around feeding, reproduction, migration, fighting, care of the plumage, social relationships, and roosting. Instincts are inherited from their parents, and have evolved through many generations. The instinctive courtship behaviour is especially important as an aid to selecting mates of the correct species.

Owls have the ability to look straight ahead in the same way as human beings. Their enormous eyes have been developed to allow maximum vision for hunting in darkness.

Feeding and Digestion

A habitat will sustain a number of different species of birds, provided that they are species that do not compete with each other. Each species has its own requirements in food, its own feeding methods, and its own nesting and feeding sites.

Feeding Habits

Within the cover of bushes and trees in a habitat, several species of insectivorous feeders may forage, each selecting favoured areas between the ground scrub layer and the upper canopy of the largest trees. Certain birds are very specialized in their feeding habits, the crossbill group being an excellent example: parrot and Scottish crossbills feed principally on pine seeds, common crossbills on larch. Their bills have adapted to cope with extracting the seeds from the cones. All these species have the tips of the mandibles crossed to prise open the cone, but the parrot crossbill has the stoutest bill and the two-barred crossbill the slimmest to cope with the cones they favour.

Even by just watching birds in the garden, the observer will soon realize how they favour particular feeding spots. Dunnocks forage on the ground under cover of bushes, wrens creep along the bases of walls peering into nooks and crannies, and warblers explore higher up in bushes looking for insects amongst the leaves. Waterfowl are another interesting group to study in this respect. Each species favours particular areas of a lake, depending on water depth and the available sources of food.

Swallowing Food

Birds have no teeth, though some species of fish-eating birds have serrated edges to their mandibles which aid them in holding their prey before it is swallowed. Food is swallowed whole or may be broken up inside the bill (seeds cracked by finch-like birds, husks discarded), or held by the foot and pieces torn away and swallowed (hawks). A few birds may even make use of 'tools' to help them break food up. Song thrushes smash snail shells on a suitable stone, and gulls drop shellfish onto rocks.

Food is swallowed into the crop where it may be kept for a short time if the bird is carrying food to its young. Some species will then regurgitate the partially digested contents into the young birds' mouths.

Digestion

Unlike mammals, birds do not have a true stomach. Instead, they have a gizzard, which is largest in birds that live on grain or other hard vegetable matter. The gizzard contains small stones (grit) which the bird has swallowed to help it crush its vegetable food. Birds of prey have no gizzard; but a series of glands help break down the flesh that is taken in.

The digested food then passes into the duodenum, and on to the various organs that process the matter and break it down even further; these are the liver, pancreas, and gall bladder. The food passes into the small intestine, which may be very long in vegetarian birds.

Digestion continues through absorption, and the waste matter is excreted through the cloaca, where waste from the kidneys is also excreted.

Reed warblers feeding young. The parents have to work hard to keep up with the demands of the young birds. On each visit to the nest, an adult will wait to collect a sac of faecal waste, which is carried away. If it were left near the nest, the white material might advertise the birds' presence to predators.

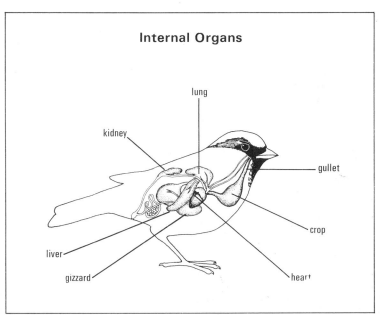

Internal Organs

lung

kidney

gullet

crop

liver

heart

gizzard

Pellets

A pellet is a lump of indigestible food items that the bird ejects through its mouth. Pellets are most well known in relation to birds of prey and owls, and afford an interesting study of the creatures on which these birds prey. Many other birds produce pellets, but those of the smaller birds may be hard to find unless birds are actually seen coughing pellets up. Searching below roosting perches is the easiest way of finding the pellets of larger birds; although they may also be found below other favourite perches.

Contents

Depending on the species or the type of food eaten, the contents of a pellet can be dissected and the prey items identified; though, obviously, many of the components are not readily recognized by the layman. The pellet may contain fur, bones, and insect wingcases, as well as other odds and ends such as feathers, hard shells of some seeds, corn husks, and stalks.

Dissection and Study

Pellets should be soaked in a dish of warm water and the contents gently prised apart with a pair of forceps. The larger items, such as skulls, may be fairly easily identified with the aid of a magnifying glass and a reference book; several books on mammals give keys to the identification of the small mammal remains that are often found in bird of prey pellets.

The larger remains may be glued to a sheet of card, and notes taken on the number and identity of small mammals found in each pellet. The results are quite interesting, and many mammalogists discover the species of small mammals found in certain areas by collecting and examining pellets. The study of an individual owl's diet, based on information gained by collecting

An eagle owl pellet containing the indigestible bones, fur, and feathers of its prey.

A dissected eagle owl's pellet. It is easy to identify the contents of this type of pellet by examining the skulls of animals found in them.

Rook pellets contain a high proportion of vegetable matter; stems and husks of corn, and small stones, known as 'grit', that are swallowed to aid digestion.

pellets from below its roost during the course of several years, can give an immense amount of useful information. It may, for example, be possible to relate the variation in small mammal populations to the breeding success of the owl.

Insect remains in pellets are generally not easy to identify unless they can be passed on to an entomologist who is interested in the subject. The beginner is advised to start off by getting to know the small mammal remains in bird of prey pellets before attempting to sort out anything more complex.

Preserving Pellets

The preservation of intact pellets is rather difficult, because they are prone to attack by mites and small moths which destroy the fur or feather components. There are even specific types of fungi that will grow only on pellets from certain types of birds.

Territories

For survival, birds require definite territories in which to live. The size of a bird's territory depends on a number of factors relating to its social and feeding habits.

Categories

Territories fall into several categories. One type is that in which birds nest and feed within the bounds of a small area of land – as in the case of robins and most other garden birds. Another type is where a bird nests in a small territory but leaves its boundaries to find food: this applies to some of the finches. Other birds, especially colonial nesting birds, have a very small area of territory around the nest itself, but feed in communal or loose flocks. Many seabirds have this type of territory.

Outside the breeding season, these territories break down. But a few species retain winter feeding territories, though this is not so prevalent in migratory birds. Robins have winter territories, but may be more tolerant of winter intruders than they would be of intruders in the breeding season. Another type of territory is simply a feeding area that birds defend against intruders. It may extend only within lunging distance of the bird itself, or may be a few metres of ideal feeding habitat.

Purpose and Size

The main object of territories is to ensure that a bird has enough food

Nesting seabirds have a minute amount of territory. Each nest may be just within pecking distance of the next. Gannets choose the largest ledges on which to build their nests; kittiwakes select the short, broad ledges; and guillemots nest on the narrowest ones.

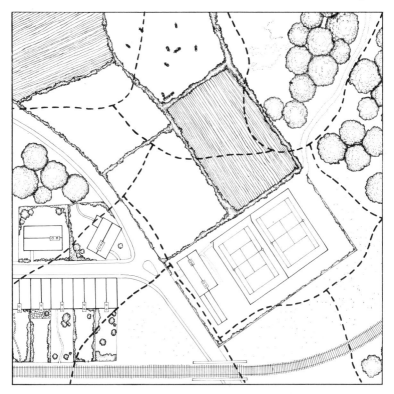

available to feed itself or its family without competing with others of the same species. Normally, they are defended by the male, who uses his brighter plumage and song to show his presence to would-be intruders, be they male or female. But females will also chase away intruding females once breeding has commenced.

The size of a territory depends to a certain extent on the population density of the species concerned, and the aggressiveness of the individual bird. In areas of low population density, each territory is larger than in areas where the species is more numerous.

By marking on a large-scale map the sightings of a bird such as the robin, a picture can be built up of the extent of each individual pair's territory.

Choice of Territories

The strongest or most successful individuals take up prime habitat in their territory. This forces the younger birds or the less successful ones to select poorer habitats. Competition therefore ensures that nature's rule of 'survival of the fittest' is best for the species.

Individual birds will return annually to select the same territory. But the precise boundaries may be a matter of dispute.

Courtship

Song plays an important part in the formation of territory and the attraction of a mate. But something further is needed and courtship displays are crucial to successful mating with the correct species.

Plumage and Colour

Many birds develop a special plumage for the breeding season – brighter colours, tufts of feathers, or bare skin about the face which becomes enlarged and colourful. These attractions are shown off to the potential mate, who responds with display postures that excite the other bird even more.

Courtship Displays

Some species have a very elaborate display. The male great bustard draws its head back onto its mantle, inflates its neck and reverses its wing feathers. The tail is fanned and brought up over its back so that the bird looks twice its normal size. Black grouse males gather into small

Rooks are gregarious birds with fairly complicated behaviour patterns. During the breeding season, the pairs acknowledge each other at the nest by bowing and cawing. The female incubates, but both partners feed the young.

groups to display at each other. They elevate their lyre-shaped tails, which are supported by the fluffed-out white under-tail coverts; then they jump at each other, kicking with their feet and leaping into the air whilst the females watch. This type of communal display is known as 'lekking'. The site of the display ground may be used for many years; this is the 'lek'.

Even the dullest-coloured birds have a form of display. Dunnocks flick their wings as they hop about after the females.

Courtship displays continue even after the nest has been built, because it reinforces the pair bond between the sexes. Feeding of the female by the male is also a feature of the courtship of many birds, and is probably a rehearsal of feeding the incubating mate on the nest, or

The courtship behaviour of the great crested grebe involves a series of ritual displays. First, the suitor approaches with arched wings.

The birds face each other with erect necks and begin an involved form of head-wagging, using elaborate side-to-side movements.

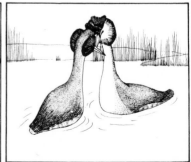

Both birds rise up on their rear ends in the water, paddling hard to maintain balance. They often carry weed in their bills.

As a final gesture, when the head-wagging and display is exhausted, the male grebe may swim to the female, offering her a fish.

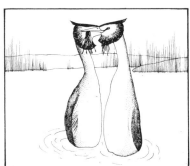

the young birds. Courtship feeding has been linked with the act of copulation; and it is interesting to note that young birds begging for food adopt a position similar to that of the female prior to coition.

Displays are particularly important where the two sexes are similar to each other in plumage. A male defending his territory will display at an intruder to obtain a response. If it receives a female display in return, the pair are on their way to forming a bond for breeding. If it is another male, there will be threat displays and some fighting – though fights rarely end in any form of injury.

Other Displays

There are other forms of display, apart from courtship. Threat displays and fighting may occur outside the breeding season over feeding territories. Ground-nesting birds often adopt a distraction-display to lead an intruding predator away from their nests. They pretend to have a broken wing – flapping away, calling loudly, trailing a wing – until the intruder has been successfully lured away from the vicinity of the nest. They then fly off to safety.

Length of Pairing

Some birds, members of the crow family and swans, for example, pair for life and rarely leave each other's company. Others mate for the single breeding season. Some species, especially Arctic-breeding waterfowl, will pair up while still in their winter quarters. As a result, they do not have to waste time finding a mate once they have reached their breeding grounds, which may have a short summer.

Male black grouse, known as blackcock, display at their 'lekking' grounds. These are traditional display grounds where each bird defends a small area called a 'court'. It is quite normal for cocks to show off to each other; their success at this proves their status within the group.

Kittiwakes greet their mates by bowing and calling – often before the mate has arrived at the nest site.

Eggs

Mammals are one of the few groups of animals that keep the developing young inside the mother's body. Birds, like most other animal groups, lay eggs and incubate them until the young are born – that is until they hatch.

Colour and Pattern

The eggs of birds vary in pattern. Many are beautifully marked and coloured, although hole-nesting species normally lay white or whitish unmarked eggs. The eggs of most ground-nesting birds, with the exception of most waterfowl, are patterned on a brownish background as an aid to camouflage. They resemble pebbles or dried vegetation in pattern.

Although there is often some variation in colour or pattern in eggs of a particular species, it seems that some birds lay eggs with an individual pattern. This is particularly true of some of the crows.

The cuckoo has a tremendous variety of colour and patterns on its eggs. The reason is that each female cuckoo specializes in selecting a foster species for its young, and lays an egg similar in colour to that of the foster birds.

Shape

Eggs vary in shape from being almost round (elliptical) to pear-shaped (pyriform). The latter type is fairly well pointed at one end and rounded at the other. It is most frequent in the case of waders, which lay their eggs on bare ground, and some of the auks, which lay eggs on cliff ledges. Because of its shape, the pyriform egg spins rather than rolls if it is disturbed by the bird moving onto or away from the nest site, and consequently it is less liable to break.

Size

The smallest egg in the world belongs to the bee hummingbird; it is not much larger than a large garden pea. The largest is laid by the ostrich and is about 170 mm in length. The kiwi lays the largest egg for its size – weighing about a quarter of its own body weight.

Number

Clutch size also varies tremendously. The game-birds and waterfowl normally have large numbers of young, many of which are lost to predators during the vulnerable period before the young birds are able to fend for themselves. Certain birds which are less prone to predation only lay one egg; this is true of many of the larger seabirds, some of which also live to a good age.

Egg Structure

The egg contains the embryo, attached to the nutritious yolk and, by means of an umbilical stalk, to a breathing membrane. There are small chambers within the egg to hold the excretions of the developing chick, as well as an air chamber that helps to control the temperature of the egg whilst under incubation. The albumen of the egg acts as a cushion for the yolk. The egg is surrounded by a hard shell, which is porous to allow the chick to breathe.

A cuckoo's egg in a reed warbler's nest. On hatching, the young cuckoo will push the other nestlings out. The foster parents then have to rear one enormous, demanding youngster.

An avocet settles down to incubate its clutch. Its long legs are folded carefully as it lowers itself onto the nest.

The nest and eggs of the little ringed plover. The eggs of wading birds are camouflaged to resemble stones. The nest consists of a hollow made by the body of the bird, lined sparsely with pieces of shell or grass. The young birds leave the nest soon after hatching.

Nesting Boxes

The population of many hole-nesting birds can be increased in areas where natural holes are not easily found, if boxes are provided for the birds to build their nests in. These boxes are quite easy to construct, and they provide much enjoyment for people who put them in their gardens. But it must be remembered that observations should be made from a distance and the contents inspected only infrequently.

There are several types of nest boxes, including the conventional tit boxes and boxes with more of an open front that may be used by robins. Even artificial nests for house martins are available on the market. Barrels, partly cut away, make ideal nest boxes for owls.

Construction

A box should have a removable lid, to enable the contents to be cleaned out at the end of the breeding season. Many parasites will pass the winter in the nest debris, and they could infect birds using the box in the following season. The box should be sited away from direct sunlight, and the floor should have a small gap to allow water to drain away during wet weather. To prevent sparrows from taking over a box, the hole should have a diameter of only 28mm. House sparrows will be unable to squeeze through.

Putting up nest boxes is a useful project for schools. Schemes to erect boxes in local woods or in the grounds of old people's homes are always worthwhile.

Right: A nest box for small tits, tree sparrows, and pied flycatchers. A metal shield should be nailed around the nest hole to prevent grey squirrels from eating eggs or young birds.

Right, below: Tawny, and barn owls will use nest boxes erected in woodland. Care should be taken that grey squirrels do not take over these boxes for their dreys.

Below: Nest boxes, suitable for house martins, can be purchased. The birds can live quite happily using a mixture of natural and artificial nests.

Attracting Birds to the Garden

Many people take great delight in seeing birds in their gardens, and there are many ways to improve a garden to create a variety of breeding and feeding places for them.

Several factors have to be taken into account before a decision is made to attract breeding birds: the size of the garden, the frequency with which it is used by children, and whether or not there are cats in it. Breeding birds need a certain amount of seclusion and may well leave nests if they are being disturbed by playing children or marauding cats. Young birds are particularly vulnerable.

Most of the species now breeding in gardens are woodland birds, and shrubby cover is important to them. There should be a certain amount of undergrowth, such as bramble patches, and weed patches are very attractive to finches – even if rather unsightly to the tidy gardener. A good policy is to pile trimmings from bushes in a quiet corner and train some bramble sprays to grow over them. This will give ideal cover for dunnocks and wrens to forage or even breed in. In natural woodland,

During winter months birds rely on a regular food source. A bird table should be kept well stocked with such items as mixed seeds, household scraps, and rotting apples. Greenfinches and tits particularly enjoy nut feeders.

there will be small open areas; these can be simulated in a garden by a mown lawn, which is very attractive to thrushes.

Birds have adapted to feed on or about native trees and plants, because these support a greater variety of insect life. Planting of native trees is preferable to ornamental ones in this respect, and the ideal bird garden should include such species as elder, birch, hawthorn, alder, or willow.

Berry-bearing trees and shrubs are very useful for birds in late autumn and winter. Berberis, cotoneaster, and sorbus species all produce good crops of berries which are attractive to thrushes; and even waxwings turn up in gardens to feed on them.

A small shallow pond will be used for drinking and bathing. Stones should be placed in it for birds to perch on. Water is especially important in winter, when many ponds are frozen; at this time, a small garden pool can be kept free of ice for the birds to use.

Feeding birds artificially is also important in winter when natural foods may be hard to find. But it is

Water should be provided for drinking and bathing. Rocks placed in a small pool provide suitable perches for birds entering the water, But care must be taken that the water does not freeze in winter.

important to keep up a regular supply, because birds will come to rely on it to keep themselves going. Giving food to birds during the breeding season should be discouraged, as natural foods, especially insects, are more nutritious to young birds; and household scraps may even be harmful to them at this stage. Mixed seeds for wild birds may be obtained from pet shops or through advertisements in bird magazines. It is much cheaper to buy seed in bulk than in small packets. Household scraps, too, are welcome in winter. A variety of nut baskets to hang from bird tables or branches is available from pet shops. Watching the antics of feeding birds on them can be most amusing.

Bird tables can be easily constructed. A collar around the upright of the table will prevent cats or squirrels from climbing up.

Injured Birds

Generally, there is little one can do for injured birds, unless they are simply exhausted by adverse weather conditions or have been only slightly injured in some other way An exhausted bird can be fed and kept warm and dry for a day or two, until it is lively enough to be released. Birds are often found stunned by the roadside, with no obvious sign of injury. It is a good policy to stop and pick them up, placing them in a sheltered place nearby. They will soon recover if they are merely stunned.

Broken Wings or Legs

Probably the kindest thing to do for small birds with broken wings is to have them destroyed, because they will be unable to fly properly again and will be at a disadvantage when released back into the wild. But large birds, such as swans, that are less prone to being preyed upon will survive for many years if unable to fly. The wing may be strapped to the body in a folded position until it is healed, and the bird can be kept until fit. Birds of prey should not be released with damaged wings.

A broken leg is little handicap unless the bird is long-legged. If the bird can be captured, a leg may be repaired by using a small splint: the split shaft of a large feather is ideal. The splint is bound with adhesive tape, and the bird should be kept until the break is healed.

Wounds

Minor wounds may be treated by cleansing with soap and water – but

Splinting a Broken Leg

splints

sticky tape

Strapping Up a Wing

sticky tape

sticky tape

counter balance strip of sticky tape

Warm soapy water and an old toothbrush can be used to remove oil from a seabird's feathers. Because this process destroys the waterproofing of the feathers the bird should be kept until the next moult when it will be seaworthy again. A rubber band placed carefully around the tip of the bill prevents the handler from being pecked.

not with a detergent. More serious injuries will need to be treated by a veterinary surgeon if the bird is not to be destroyed.

Ailing Birds

Birds contract many diseases, and a sick bird with no obvious sign of injury could be suffering from any one of a number of complaints. A common one is pesticide poisoning. If the bird allows itself to be caught, it is probably in a bad way and should be destroyed.

Oiled Birds

Unfortunately, a fairly common sight on beaches today is a bird covered in oil. Such a bird should be taken to a local society that helps animals and that will know what to do. Oiled seabirds can be cleaned, but cleaning destroys the waterproofing in their plumage.

Orphaned Young Birds

Fledglings seen on the ground often appear to have been abandoned by their parents. Generally, they have not been abandoned at all but are merely learning to fly. They should be left where they are or placed in a safe place nearby. They should not be taken away: it is very hard to rear a young bird and to feed it properly.

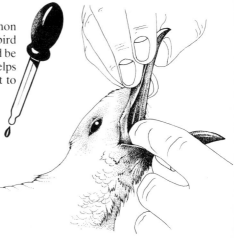

Most wild birds, if they are injured, have to be 'force-fed'. With a small bird, the upper mandible can be lifted with the finger nails and tiny pieces of food pushed well down the bird's gullet. Water can be given using a dropper.

113

Conservation

The clearance of land for building or for agricultural use has resulted in the destruction of many wildlife habitats throughout the world. Forests have been felled, deserts irrigated, wetlands drained, and seas and rivers polluted. Much of the earth's land surface is cultivated for food crops, and overgrazing by domesticated animals has destroyed much natural vegetation. Many forms of animal and plant life have become very rare as a result, and some have become extinct.

Gradually, people have become aware of the need to protect and save wildlife for future generations to enjoy. In many countries, there are active conservation organizations, some of which are run by governments, but others of which depend on membership subscriptions for finance. At first sight, there may seem to be too many; but each works in a different field of protection or wildlife management. Locally, there may be naturalists' trusts running small reserves that hold rare plants or interesting areas

Conservation workers clear dense thickets of rhododendron. Having taken a strong hold, the species threatens the growth of natural woodlands. The shrubs are cut and burned, and the stumps treated with a chemical to prevent new shoots forming.

An extensive monoculture of damp grassland is improved by creating small pools. This is often done by the use of explosives.

of habitat. The national organizations have larger reserves: in Britain, Europe's largest voluntary conservation organization, the Royal Society for the Protection of Birds (RSPB), administers more than 100 reserves and has over 390,000 members.

Managing a Reserve

It is not enough to set aside an area of land as a nature reserve and just leave it alone; it has to be managed in rather the same way as a garden has to be managed. Otherwise, certain dominant plants will take over and choke out other species that were present in the first place.

But, carefully managed, land can become a more interesting habitat for wildlife. This may involve a certain amount of destruction of bushes that have encroached on it to open up areas for the establishment of undergrowth. Or patches may have to be cleared in reed beds in order to create some open pools. And alien plants may have to be destroyed in order to bring about a better balance of native vegetation.

Habitat management is quite a complex affair. The area concerned should be adequately surveyed before any work is undertaken, in order that the plant and animal life may be understood. Then aims and ideals can be worked out and the work commenced.

Voluntary Help

There is always a need for voluntary help in managing reserves; though, of course, there will also be professionals working too. The best way to get involved in conservation work is to contact a local society and find out what is going on near by.

The water levels on low-lying fields liable to flood can be controlled by sluices. In winter, a field can be allowed to flood, and the water drained off again in the spring for the breeding season. The flood conditions are particularly useful to flocks of wintering waterfowl, as they can feed on the numerous plant seeds that are washed to the surface.

Conservation Laws

Many forms of animal and plant life are now protected in some way in most countries. Various conservation laws can affect the birdwatcher, and it is advisable to find out what restrictions apply in any particular place. Infringements can involve heavy penalties.

Classification

There have been several attempts at classifying the world's birds: the one most universally accepted is the Wetmore Sequence, which was proposed by Alexander Wetmore in 1930. It follows a hypothetical evolutionary sequence, starting with the ostrich and ending with the perching birds (passerines).

There are some 8,600 different species of birds in the world, the great majority of them in the tropics where evolution has produced a greater variety of all living things. About 650 species are known to have occurred in Europe, of which 450 are of regular occurrence.

All known living organisms have been given scientific names, with Latin or Greek derivations, which are used internationally. This is useful when dealing with biologists in other parts of the world. For example, the dunlin is known in North America as the *red-backed sandpiper*; in France it is the *becasseau variable*; and it has numerous other names throughout the world. However, its scientific name is *Calidris alpina*, and by this name it will be known to biologists throughout the world.

The first part of the name is the Genus, the second the specific part of the name. The dunlin shares the Genus *Calidris* with several other similar species, such as the little stint, which is *Calidris minuta*. Over different parts of the world-distribution of a bird, evolution can produce small differences, but a bird from one place is identifiable when compared to others of the same species from elsewhere. These differences may call for the species to be split into subspecies; and when subspecies are referred to, the name will be in three parts.

Although the genus *Calidris* contains several species, it is different in many respects from other wader species. Several genera may be grouped together in a family, in this case the *Scolopacidae*. Grouping can be taken still further by lumping families together under Orders.

European birds may be grouped into the following Orders. The number of regular species in each family is given.

A species may sometimes vary enough within its range to be split into subspecies. The very slight differences of markings among subspecies can prove a problem to the birdwatcher. The grey-headed wagtail, left, from Scandinavia is a member of the yellow wagtail species. The blue-headed wagtail, right, is found in all other parts of Europe. The latter has a white eye-stripe that helps to distinguish it from its Scandinavian relation.

Orders of Birds

GAVIIFORMES
Gavidae (Divers: 4)
PODICIPEDIFORMES
Podicipedidae (Grebes: 5)
PROCELLARIIFORMES
Procellariidae (Shearwaters: 6)
Hydrobatidae (Storm Petrels: 3)
PELECANIFORMES
Sulidae (Gannets: 1)
Phalacrocoracidae (Cormorants: 3)
Pelecanidae (Pelecans: 2)
CICONIIFORMES
Ardeidae (Herons: 9)
Ciconiidae (Storks: 2)
Threskiornithidae (Ibises: 2)
PHOENICOPTERIFORMES
Phoenicopteridae (Flamingoes: 1)
ANSERIFORMES
Anatidae (Ducks: 45)
ACCIPITRIFORMES
Accipitridae (Hawks: 27)
Pandionidae (Osprey: 1)
FALCONIFORMES
Falconidae (Falcons: 10)
GALLIFORMES
Tetraonidae (Grouse: 5)
Phasiandiae (Partridges: 7)
GRUIFORMES
Turnicidae (Hemipodes: 1)
Rallidae (Rails: 9)
Gruidae (Cranes: 2)
Otididae (Bustards: 2)
CHARADRIIFORMES
Haematopodidae (Oystercatchers: 1)
Recurvirostridae (Avocets: 2)
Burhinidae (Stone Curlews: 1)
Glareolidae (Pratincoles: 2)
Charadriidae (Plovers: 8)
Scolopacidae (Sandpipers: 32)
Stercorariidae (Skuas: 4)
Laridae (Gulls: 14)
Sternidae (Terns: 10)
Alcidae (Auks: 6)
PTEROCLIDIFORMES

Pteroclididae (Sandgrouse: 2)
COLUMBIFORMES
Columbidae (Doves: 6)
CUCULIFORMES
Cuculidae (Cuckoos: 2)
STRIGIFORMES
Tytonidae (Barn Owls: 1)
Strigidae (Owls: 12)
CAPRIMULGIFORMES
Caprimulgidae (Nightjars: 2)
APODIFORMES
Apodidae (Swifts: 4)
CORACIIFORMES
Alcedinidae (Kingfishers: 1)
Meropidae (Bee-eaters: 1)
Coraciidae (Rollers: 1)
Upupidae (Hoopoe: 1)
PICIFORMES
Picidae (Woodpeckers: 10)
PASSERIFORMES
Alaudidae (Larks: 9)
Hirundinidae (Swallows: 5)
Motacillidae (Pipits: 10)
Bombycillidae (Waxwings: 1)
Cinclidae (Dippers: 1)
Trogodytidae (Wrens: 1)
Prunellidae (Accentors: 2)
Turdidae (Thrushes: 24)
Sylviidae (Warblers: 38)
Muscicapidae (Flycatchers: 5)
Timaliidae (Babblers: 1)
Aegithalidae (Long-tailed Tits: 1)
Paridae (Tits: 8)
Sittidae (Nuthatches: 3)
Tichodromadidae (Wall Creepers: 1)
Certhiidae (Tree Creepers: 2)
Remizidae (Penduline Tits: 1)
Oriolidae (Orioles: 1)
Laniidae (Shrikes: 5)
Corvidae (Crows: 11)
Sturnidae (Starlings: 3)
Passeridae (Sparrows: 5)
Estrildidae (Waxbills: 1)
Fringillidae (Finches: 20)
Emberizidae (Buntings: 14)

Bird Watcher's Calendar

During the course of the year many events happen that vary the species or numbers of birds likely to be seen.

January

Lakes, reservoirs, and estuaries are used by flocks of waterfowl and waders throughout the winter. There is little evidence of bird movements, unless there is some cold weather – then, large numbers of lapwings, skylarks, thrushes, wood pigeons, and waterfowl will move on.

February

Some evidence of movement can be detected, with increasing numbers of gulls arriving on estuaries and inland reservoirs. Flocks of finches are still feeding in farmyards and stubble fields. Many birds are in song, starting to form territories. Wildfowl are displaying and pairing up before moving north. Herons, crows, and some garden birds start nest building if the weather is fine.

March

Increasing numbers of waders on coasts and estuaries as birds arrive from farther south. The first wheatears, sand martins, and chiffchaffs are arriving from mid-month. Bird song increases and partridges and lapwings are calling and displaying. Flocks of finches and buntings are breaking up to set up territory.

April

The breeding season for many birds is now in full swing. Arriving summer migrants are in good numbers, with many other birds moving through the countryside *en route* for farther north. Most winter visitors have left by the end of the month.

May

Many summer migrants are now breeding and the countryside is full of song. Further species arrive. Swifts are coming into the country during the first half of the month. There is a marked passage of finches along the coast. Overshooting migrants arriving on coasts can include rarities. Coastal cliffs are bustling with breeding seabirds.

June

The estuaries are virtually deserted by waders. Most passage has now finished, but there is a good chance of rare vagrants on the coast. Moorlands are now active with displaying curlew and golden plover. Many young birds are learning to fly. Lapwings are starting to flock and moving away from the edges of moorlands.

July

Some waders are now coming back onto estuaries. Young seabirds are leaving cliffs. Towards the end of the month, a few migrant small birds move along the coast. Most birds are now quiet and moulting.

August

Flocks of moulting waterfowl have been gathering on inland lakes, and shelduck have departed to moult in Heligoland Bight. Waders are now passing in large numbers. Moorlands are much quieter, deserted by

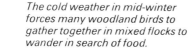

In August, moorland-nesting waders may start to form flocks. The golden plover moves from its moorland breeding ground to an estuary or low-lying field.

The cold weather in mid-winter forces many woodland birds to gather together in mixed flocks to wander in search of food.

breeding waders. Many migrants of all types are found along coastlines.

September

Wader passage drops towards the end of the month. Waterfowl numbers start to increase on wintering waters. Many migrant small birds are on the move, with 'falls' of large numbers at coastal sites. The first of the winter thrushes start to arrive on the east coast and move inland.

October

Winter visitors, especially thrushes, are now arriving in large numbers with easterly winds, and a few vagrants from central Asia turn up along east and south coasts under the same conditions. Flocks of waterfowl are building up on lakes. Wintering waders are found in large numbers on estuaries. Tawny owls start hooting again. There are flocks of finches and larks in stubbles and farmyards, and redpolls and siskins on alders and birches. All summer visitors have departed.

November

Redwings and fieldfares are stripping berries from hedges. In good years, waxwings turn up along eastern coasts. Bramblings, often mixed with chaffinches, feed in flocks on fallen beech mast. Large roosts form of thrushes, rooks, jackdaws, and starlings. Woodland birds gather into mixed flocks to roam through the trees.

December

There is little movement: winter birds are ensconced in their winter quarters unless there are periods of cold weather that cause many birds to fly to milder areas. Some bird song has now started if the weather is mild. Large numbers of gulls gather to roost on inland lakes and estuaries. Guillemots start visiting their breeding cliffs.

Glossary

Aberrant A bird that is in an unusual state of plumage, making it appear different from the normal type.

Abrasion The effect of wear on feathers, often showing in the markings about the edges of the wing. Feathers are worn away through abrasion.

Accipiter A genus of hawk. The term is often used to refer to an unidentified bird which is either a sparrowhawk or a goshawk.

Adult A bird that has reached its definitive plumage and is capable of breeding.

Albino Lacking pigment, through genetic abnormality or due to age or an accident. True albinos are rare; they are white with pink eyes and skin, but partial albinos, with white patches, may be seen.

Albumen The 'white' of an egg.

Allopatric Where the ranges of two closely related species replace each other without overlapping.

Allopreening Term used when two birds preen each other.

Altricial Young birds that are hatched blind and naked; an alternative term is *nidicolous*.

Auk A family of seabirds. The term is also used in relation to distant unidentifiable birds that may be razorbills, guillemots, or puffins.

Avian The class of animals known as birds are referred to in scientific terms as *aves*. Anything to do with birds is *avian*.

Aviculture The keeping of birds in captivity.

Avifauna The bird life of a defined area.

Axillaries The feathers at the base of the underside of the wings: the 'armpit'.

Banding See RINGING.

Barb Part of the vane of a feather.

Bill The beak of the bird.

Biomass An ecological term referring to the number of organisms on a specified area of land.

Birder American term for 'birdwatcher'.

Bonxie Alternative name for great skua.

Brood Collective term for a nest of young.

Buteo A genus of buzzards; a specifically unidentifiable buzzard may be referred to in this way.

Carpal The bend of the wing. It appears to be the 'elbow' of the wing but is in fact the 'wrist'.

Cere Bare skin about the base of the bill, as in birds of prey.

Chat Group references to smaller members of the thrush family, namely wheatear, stonechat, robin, or redstart type birds.

Cline Throughout the world range of a species there may be differences so gradual that clear divisions cannot be made. This type of gradation is a cline.

Clutch The set of eggs that exists when a bird has finished laying and is incubating.

Commensal feeding Where different species feed together and the activities of one indirectly helps the other.

Conspecific Subspecies that have been lumped into one species, though they may look rather different.

Corvid A member of the crow family; the term may be used with reference to an unidentifiable dark member of this family.

Covey Collective noun for a party of partridges.

Crepuscular Active at twilight – that is, at dawn and dusk.

Cryptic Term used to describe patterns of plumage that afford concealment and camouflage.

Culmen The ridge along the top of a bird's bill.

Decoy Either an artificial bird placed to attract wild birds, such as waterfowl, onto a pond, or an elaborate form of trap constructed to catch waterfowl.

Dimorphism A term used to describe two or more constant colour forms of a bird.

Dispersal The spreading-out of a bird population from a point of origin.

Distal Farthest from the point of attachment; used chiefly when describing bill and tail colour patterns.

Diurnal Active during daylight hours.

Drift A term used to describe a shift by migrating birds away from their normal migration route; it is often caused by weather conditions.

Dust bathing Many birds take delight in bathing in powdery soil – presumed to help in freeing the plumage from parasites.

Eclipse plumage A stage of plumage that male ducks moult into after the end of the breeding season; in *eclipse* they are dull-coloured and resemble the females. The colourful male dress is acquired again in the early winter.

Ectoparasite Parasite living on the outside of a bird's body.

Emargination The 'cut away' shapes of the outer webs of the primaries in many birds; it may be very important in identifying some warblers in the hand.

Endemic Restricted to a defined area.

Endoparasite Parasite living inside a bird's body.

Eyas A nestling falcon.

Eyrie The nest of a large bird of prey.

Fall A term used to describe the situation when a number of migrant birds are forced to land following inclement weather.

Feral A formerly domestic species that has gone 'wild'.

Gaggle Collective noun for a flying party of geese.

Gander A male goose.

Gape The inside of the mouth and bill; in fledglings the gape may be brightly coloured to attract the attention of the returning adult bird carrying food.

Genus The scientific term for a group of closely related species.

Gizzard Part of the stomach of a bird.

Gonad The sex organs, being the testes of the male and the ovary of the female.

Gonys The angle along the lower mandible, particularly notable in the larger gulls.

Grit Small stones that are swallowed by the bird and held in the gizzard to help digestion.

Gular pouch Bare skin about the throat, as in pelicans.

Gullet The forepart of the oesophagus in the throat of the bird.

Heligoland trap A construction for trapping birds, originally used on the island of Heligoland and still in use at some bird observatories. It is a large funnel-like construction of wire-netting on a frame.

Holarctic The Palearctic and Nearctic Faunal Region combined.

Hybrid A cross between two species. It is comparatively rare in the wild, but a frequent occurrence in captivity where birds are kept in unnaturally close conditions.

Immature A term applied to plumages other than fully adult.

Indigenous A species that is native to a described area.

Invasion A sudden expansion of a bird's range into areas where it is not normally found.

Irruption See INVASION.

Jaeger American name for the skuas.

Jesses Straps placed on the legs of birds of prey by falconers for handling purposes. Escaped birds of prey may be wearing them.

Juvenile Name given to the first true covering of feathers a bird has after leaving the nest. In some birds, juvenile plumage may be identifiable as late as the following winter, in which case it may be referred to as 'first-winter'.

Kinglet Family name for goldcrest and firecrest.

Lek A display ground for certain species, such as black grouse and ruff.

Leucistic A form of abnormal plumage, the colour of which is very pale but not white.

Loon American name for the divers.

Lure A form of bait used by falconers whilst training their birds; or an instrument used for imitating bird calls.

Malar Relating to the side of the throat.

Mandible A bird's bill is in two parts, the upper and lower mandibles.

Milk Pigeons and doves feed their nestlings on a substance that resembles milk or cheese. It is regurgitated into the young birds' mouths, and is known as *pigeon's milk*.

Mimicry Many birds will imitate sounds made by other birds and incorporate them into their own songs.

Mist nets Fine mesh nets used by trained ringers to catch birds for study.

Mobbing Birds of prey, crows, and other predatory birds may be chased by smaller birds in an attempt to move them away from their territories.

Mollymauk Name often given to the smaller species of albatross, including the black-browed albatross.

Mule A term used in aviculture for a cross between a canary and another finch.

Murre American name for the guillemots.

Nares The nostrils of a bird.

Nearctic The North American Faunal Region.

Nictitating membrane A membrane which can cover the exterior of the eye for cleaning purposes or protection; almost a transparent third eyelid.

Nidicolous See ALTRICIAL.

Nidifugous See PRECOCIAL.

Nocturnal Active at night.

Observatory Coastal stations which have been set up to study bird migration by daily counts and ringing. Hostel-type accommodation is normally provided for visitors who book in advance.

Oil gland An organ situated on the lower back which produces secretions used by birds whilst preening; the precise function is not clearly known.

Oology The study of birds' eggs.

Orbital ring A ring of differently coloured feathers around the eye.

Order A taxonomic category which contains a number of closely-related families.

Ornithology The study of birds.

Palearctic Faunal Region of North Africa, Europe, and Asia, north of the tropics. It may be divided into the West Palearctic and the East Palearctic.

Palmate Having three toes connected by webs.

Passerine Perching birds of the order *Passeriformes*.

Peck order A social order evolved within a group of colonial or social birds: the dominant bird or animal is at the top of the peck order.

Pectoral The breast region of a bird.

Peewit Alternative name for *lapwing*.

Pelagic Normally inhabiting the oceans.

Pellet A lump of indigestible food matter ejected through a bird's mouth.

Phase A colour form within a species.

Pinioning Rendering a captive bird incapable of flying by cutting one wing at the carpal joint and preventing future growth of the primaries.

Precocial Young birds that are active soon after hatching and are covered in down. Alternative name is *nidifugous*.

Pullus A young bird, still in the nest.

Rectrices The tail feathers; singular, *retrix*.

Reeve A female ruff.

Relict populations Isolated populations of a species that was probably more widespread at one time.

Remiges The main flight feathers, the primaries and secondaries; singular, *remex*.

Reverse migration The phenomenon of some birds migrating in the opposite direction to the norm. The causes are not accurately known but, mostly, young birds are involved and it may be associated with weather conditions at the time of migration.

Ringing Also known as *banding* in North America. The study of birds by trapping them and placing small numbered rings on their legs. Much is learnt about migration, population, breeding success, survival rate, and longevity by ringing.

Sibling species Two or more species that are very similiar but separated geographically.

Species A term used in classifying birds (or other animals). It is best defined by saying that any particular species of bird does not normally interbreed with other species; through evolution each species has become reproductively isolated from other similar types.

Subspecies Populations of birds that differ from each other within a species but freely interbreed where populations overlap.

Sympatric Where closely related species overlap each other's range without interbreeding.

Taxonomy The study of the relationships between species and subspecies, and their classification.

Tiercel The male falcon.

Tystie Alternative name for *black guillemot*.

Vagrant A wandering bird discovered far outside its normal range.

Zygodactyl Having two toes directed forward and two back.

Books to Read

The birdwatcher should aim to build up a small library of reference books. Most bookshops keep some bird books, but generally the selection is rather limited. A useful address to know is that of The Bird Bookshop, 21 Regents Terrace, Edinburgh, Scotland, which has a very comprehensive choice of books. It publishes a regular price list for postal buyers. A selection of helpful books is given here.

Identification
There are three very popular field guides; it is as well to have at least two to check identifications:
A Field Guide to the Birds of Britain and Europe by Roger Tory Peterson, Guy Mountford and P. A. D. Hollom; published by Collins.
The Kingfisher Guide to the Birds of Britain and Europe by Neil Ardley; published by Kingfisher Books.
Field Guide to the Birds of Britain and Ireland by John Gooders; published by Kingfisher Books.

For further information, the reader should consult more detailed works, such as:
The Birdlife of Britain by Peter Hayman and Philip Burton; published by Mitchell Beazley.
The Popular Handbook of British Birds by P. A. D. Hollom; published by Witherby.
Flight Identification of European Raptors by R. F. Porter, Ian Willis, Steen Christensen and Bent Pors Nielsen; published by Poyser.
Handbook of the Birds of Europe, the Middle East and North Africa. The Birds of the Western Palearctic, edited by Stanley Cramp and K. E. L. Simmons; published by Oxford University Press.

Distribution
The Atlas of Breeding Birds in Britain and Ireland by J. T. R. Sharrock; published by Poyser.
The Status of Birds in Britain and Ireland by the British Ornithologists' Union; published by Blackwell Scientific Publications.

Migration
The Palearctic-African Bird Migration Systems by R. E. Moreau; published by Academic Press

General
A New Dictionary of Birds, edited by Sir A. Landsborough Thomson; published by Nelson. This is a comprehensive work covering all aspects of ornithology.
Man and Birds by R. K. Murton; published by Collins.
Projects with Birds by Peter Goodfellow; published by David and Charles.

Sound Recording
Recording Natural History Sounds by Richard Margoschis; published by Print and Press Services Ltd.

Photography
Introduction to Bird and Wildlife Photography by John Marchington and Anthony Clay; published by Faber and Faber.
Wildlife Photography: a Field Guide by Eric Hosking and John Gooders; published by Hutchinson.

Index

The Publishers wish to thank the following for their kind help in
supplying photographs for this book:
Brian Hawkes, Eric Hosking, Steve Madge, Pat Morris.
Cover photograph: David Hosking